THE BATTLE OF BRITAIN AND THE BLITZ

VOICES FROM THE TWENTIETH CENTURY

EYEWITNESS ACCOUNTS FROM **THE IMPERIAL WAR MUSEUM** SOUND ARCHIVE

THE BATTLE OF BRITAIN AND THE BLITZ

CONSULTING EDITOR:
NIGEL FOUNTAIN

First published in Great Britain in 2002 by
Michael O'Mara Books Limited
9 Lion Yard, Tremadoc Road
London SW4 7NQ

A CIP catalogue record for this book is available from the British Library

ISBN 1-85479-856-1

1 3 5 7 9 10 8 6 4 2

Designed and typeset by Design 23

www.mombooks.com

Printed and bound in Singapore by Tien Wah Press

Cover images: background – contemporary War Office propaganda poster for the RAF; foreground left – Hulton Archive; foreground right – IWM: KY SS48E

This book has been produced with the co-operation and assistance of the Imperial War Museum, London, Britain's museum of national conflict. In particular, the consulting editor and the publishers wish to express their gratitude to the following members of the Museum's staff, for their help in preparing the text and illustrations:

Laurie Milner, senior historian with the Research and Information Department, and General Editor of the 'Voices From the Twentieth Century' series, whose idea the series was;

Margaret Brooks, Keeper of the Sound Archive, for her advice, encouragement and generous assistance over reproduction charges;

Dr Brad King, Keeper of the Department of Photographs, for generously granting permission to reproduce the Museum's images free of charge, and to the staff of the Department for their help in preparing prints;

Dr Christopher Dowling, OBE, Director of Public Services, and Elizabeth Bowers, Publications Officer, for their interest in the initial idea and for helping to bring about the Museum's involvement;

Barbara Levy, the Museum's literary agent, for her patient assistance in bringing that involvement to fruition.

Thanks also to Lynne Woolmer of River Records for providing music for the CD.

With the exception of IWM: PST 3738 (p.2) and IWM: HU 36220 (endpapers), all images provided by the Imperial War Museum are credited in brackets following each caption.

The remaining images are credited as follows:

Hulton Archive – pp. 7, 15 (below), 26, 35 (below), 36, 38, 39, 40, 63 (top left), 65 (both), 67, 73, 75 (top), 77, 81, 82, 89, 92, 93, 99, 101, 102-3 (below), 104 (top left), 106 (below), 108 (below left), 109 (below right), 110 (top left), 111, 113, 116, 117 (top), 118, 119, 120 (below), 124, 126, 127 (below), 133, 134, 136, 137, 138. **Mary Evans Picture Library** – pp.10, 19 (top & below left), 22 (below left), 23, 31, 47 (below right), 59, 70, 71, 75 (below left), 78, 83, 86, 87, 90, 94, 95, 98 (top), 102 (top left), 106 (top right), 114, 115, 122, 123 (both), 125, 141. **TRH / R Winslade** – p.42. **Atlantic Syndication** – p.135.

CONTENTS

Author Acknowledgements

It was Toby Buchan and Gabrielle Mander at Michael O'Mara Books who crystallized the idea of this project. Together with their colleague Helen Cumberbatch, they provided the support and enthusiasm which saw it through. Picture editor Jackum Brown, and Judith Palmer, drew many of the spectacular images from the Imperial War Museum, and Ron Callow and Simon Buchanan of Design 23 put them together with the words.

Unfailingly helpful, staff at the IWM's Sound Archive, the keeper of the archive Margaret Brooks, Richard McDonough and John Stopford-Pickering, opened up the past to me – and John showed me routes through. Margaret, together with senior interviewer Conrad Wood and the rest of that group of IWM interviewers are the people who have created a priceless insight into the history of the twentieth century.

Encouragement, and forbearance came from Monica Henriquez as I worked on the project, and my sister Marilyn Jamieson, a bombed-out child of the Southampton Blitz, gave me her recollections and insight. Without John Fordham's assistance much of the material would never have made it from transcript into computer, let alone book and CD. In Manchester the professionalism of Mike Thornton of One Stop Digital and producer Bob Dickinson made putting together the CD a pleasure.

Without the interviewees, there would have been no project. Without their extraordinary generation, the world would have been a very different, and much worse place.

INTRODUCTION

THIS BOOK IS ABOUT WHAT HAPPENED TO THE inhabitants of a cluster of grey, wet islands off the north-west coast of a continent. And it is about how people on those islands, by the act of holding on, saved the world.

In words and sound and pictures, it covers the Battle of Britain and the Blitz, during the years from the declaration of war in 1939, through the fall of France, the evacuation of Dunkirk, the Battle of Britain, the Blitz of 1940-1 and the 1944-5 missile attacks. It has a cast of millions, but only a handful – well, maybe a busload – of story-tellers to tell of those events. These are a few of the many women and men who spoke into an Imperial War Museum microphone about what they did, and what happened to them, during six years, six decades ago. Their lives – some of which are vigorously continuing – like all

lives, are but drops in the historical ocean, but they were part of an awe-inspiring wave, and, in speaking for themselves, they reveal a remarkable generation. They include people who were then evacuees, journalists, children, servicemen, servicewomen and refugees.

For me, sitting in the Imperial War Museum in south London, eyes closed, headphones on, listening to the voices which now follow, on paper and CD, was time travel, their past became a vicarious present. Royal Air Force fighter pilots Hugh Dundas, Roland Beamont, Tony Bartley and WAAF liaison officer Elizabeth Quayle spoke of the

RAF bomber crew on their return from the 1,000-plane bombing raid on Cologne, June 1942

7

Vast numbers of troops are evacuated from the burning coastline at Dunkirk. (IWM: HU 2108)

Dunkirk evacuation, and my mind, after fleetingly considering images of contemporary cross-Channel ferries, switched and refocused. It is true, the pictures are better in sound. There were the blazing oil tanks and a pillar of black smoke, seen from the air, drifting seventy-five miles down the French coastline, Allied soldiers holed up in seaside hotels along the sands; the encircling, inexorable, invincible German Army, the Stuka dive bombers, the RAF fighters, low on fuel, snatching minutes over the beaches from their bases in southern England.

Out of the past, what chilled me, safe in that twenty-first-century south London of traffic jams, pizza parlours, and circling jumbo jets, was a realization of what should have been glaringly obvious. In war the natural home of happy endings is over the rainbow. Listen to the voices of the people who lived those years between 1939 and 1945 and the world can be a terrifying place. For anyone caught up in war, a constant companion is danger and its ending may be tragedy, death, the death of loved ones.

But having time-travelled, I found myself asking awkward questions: What would I have done? What would I have thought? Would I have believed in an Allied victory? Come to that, in summer 1940, who were the Allies? And what constituted victory anyway?

Holding on was a victory. But even holding on to life, which is elemental and elementary, was difficult. There were values to hold on to as well, values kicked around and occasionally brandished in the pre-war years, like justice, democracy, honour, tolerance; words so worn by repetition that in smooth times, like now and in the 'dirty decade' of the 1930s, they can hardly get any grip on reality. And then there was one's own patch. Holding on to that, the place of one's birth, where one had been to school, fallen in love, worked, got sacked, gone hungry, done well, found happiness, suddenly became an issue. And holding on to it, assuming it was still there, involved firemen and emergency workers and neighbours like Ellen Harris's butcher; and it involved the assistance of people with strange accents who had arrived from lands devastated by Nazism: Poland, France, Czechoslovakia, Norway, Denmark, Holland, Spain, Germany, Belgium. It involved people from Canada, Australasia, the Indian subcontinent, Africa, the West Indies, the United States, black, white and brown, people for whom contact with family, friends, myths and empire had added up to a place for which it was worth risking one's life.

Safely situated sixty years further along history's road, their collective act of holding on then, their decision is taken for granted. But it was not inevitable. Listening to these voices, for me, underlined the significance of the vital weeks of May 1940. At that time the fate of the islands – and of the world – hung in the balance. There was not just the prospect of a German invasion; there was another possibility – the weary acquiescence by the British government in Hitler's triumph.

Many apparently reasonable people were disturbed by the bellicosity of the new Prime Minister Winston Churchill. His Foreign Secretary Lord Halifax desired mediation, and peace with Hitler. The German dictator, an admirer of the British Empire, desired peace as well, particularly since a decadent country with a wrecked army and an untried, clearly inadequate air force was patently in no position to resist. Winston Churchill disagreed. He was supported by the majority of the public, by the Labour and Liberal parties and, fortunately, by the man whose name was to go down as the symbol of the appeasement of Hitler, Neville Chamberlain. His support then helped win over anti-Churchill waverers within the Conservative Party.

So the British set about holding on. This involved losing a lot of battles – and hoping that something would turn up. The first thing that did do that was victory over the Luftwaffe in the Battle of Britain, thanks to technological genius, strategy and the likes of the people whose voices form the backbone of this book. Two years after that victory Churchill told the House of Commons that he had not become 'the King's First Minister in order to preside over the liquidation of the British Empire'. But that was exactly what was to happen, just as the decision to fight on in 1940 ensured that Britain would end the war in 1945 exhausted and virtually bankrupt.

It need not have happened. A deal, of sorts, could have been done between London and Berlin in 1940, but the world, east and west, would have gradually descended into a pit. In 1940 Churchill said that 'If we fail,

Victims of the Blitz gather precious belongings from bomb-damaged homes.

9

DOCTOR CARROT guards your Health

BETTER POT-LUCK
with Churchill today

THAN HUMBLE PIE
under Hitler tomorrow

DON'T WASTE FOOD!

Citizens are encouraged to take extra care of their health during war time. (IWM: PST 0713)

A war poster warns the British public about the dangers of idle talk. (IWM: PST 3722)

"........ but for Heaven's sake don't say I told you!"

CARELESS TALK COSTS LIVES

British Prime Minister Neville Chamberlain visits Adolf Hitler in Munich in 1938, on a peace mission. Amidst Hitler's broken promises, war between Britain and Germany becomes inevitable.

During the wartime ration period, posters remind the British public that food is precious and not to be wasted. (IWM: PST 3108)

then the whole world, including the United States, including all that we have known and cared for, will sink into the abyss of a New Dark Age, made more sinister, and perhaps more protracted, by the lights of perverted science.' He was assessing the consequence of defeat, but the consequence of a deal in May – and Hitler was still

Civilians build air-raid shelters to protect themselves against attacks from enemy bombs.

making his 'Last Appeal To Reason' in July – would have been much the same. In the land of might-have-beens the likelihood is that Britain would have had its own version of France's Vichy, complete with a pro-Nazi government. The draining of democracy could have been quite subtle, at first. Dr Klaus Hinrichsen, who features in this book, would have been returned to Germany and death, rather than sit through his daft detention on the Isle of Man, which the shabby 'alien' scares of 1940 had visited on him. The deportations of British citizens to death camps would have begun, Nazi invitations to join a crusade against the 'barbarians in the east' would have become steadily more insistent. A dark age would have ensued. Its shadow would still be falling over the twenty-first century.

No deal was done. No defeat or occupation took place. So the grey, wet islands survived to become the western springboard for victory. And eight-year-old Eric Hill endured the raiding bombers overhead, rather than the invaders marching along Southampton's Above Bar. Great Britain, offshore Europe, did not suffer the grim occupations of continental Europe.

But it suffered the Blitz. In 1939 and early in 1940 the RAF, and the Luftwaffe, had hung back from all-out bomber warfare against each other's cities. But as metropolises like London and Coventry were engulfed, and as nightfighter crewmen like Reginald Lewis bailed out over a blazing Liverpool, RAF Bomber Command was moving towards the mass bombing of German cities. A process that had begun on the day that war broke out in September 1939 with Ellen Harris descending into an air-raid shelter on Islington Green in north London ended with the atom-bombing of Hiroshima and Nagasaki in August 1945.

And there were glimmers of that

Hundreds of city-dwelling children are evacuated to the relative safety of the country.

'perverted science'. The V-1 flying bombs and V-2 rockets that rained on London in the concluding months of the war were, as Stanley Baron was to witness, the products of scientific minds – and slave labourers.

I listened, at the Imperial War Museum, to other witnesses to these events who do not feature in the book and CD, but whose memories have added depth and texture to what I understand of that time. And while the CD itself does not cover all the ground covered by the book, together, I hope, they reveal a fragment of the wartime lives of the interviewees and the atmosphere of that wartime society. Conversational repetitions were generally edited out, and some material was composited. But to the best of my ability, what is seen and heard is what was said by members of an heroic generation, to the Museum's inspired and diligent questioners.

CHAPTER ONE

ONE DAY – AND FIVE YEARS

ON 3 SEPTEMBER 1939 THE SEVENTY-ONE-YEAR-old Prime Minister, Neville Chamberlain, addressed the people of Great Britain, on BBC Radio.

I am speaking to you from the Cabinet Room at 10 Downing Street. This morning the British Ambassador in Berlin handed the German Government a final note stating that unless we heard from them by 11 o'clock that they were prepared at once to withdraw their troops from Poland a state of war would exist between us. I have to tell you now that no such undertaking has been received, and that consequently this country is at war with Germany. You can imagine what a bitter blow it is to me that all my long struggle to win peace has failed. Yet I cannot believe that there is anything more or anything different that I could have done and that would have been more successful. Up to the very last it would have been quite possible to have arranged a peaceful settlement between Germany and Poland. But Hitler would not have it. He had evidently made up his mind to attack Poland whatever happened, and although he now says he put forward reasonable proposals, which were rejected by the Poles, that is not a true statement. The proposals were never shown to the Poles, nor to us, and, though they were announced in a German broadcast on Thursday night, Hitler did not wait to

The *Daily Sketch* announces confirmation of war between Britain and Germany.

hear comments on them, but ordered his troops to cross the Polish frontier. His action shows convincingly that there is no chance of expecting that this man will ever give up his practice of using force to gain his will. He can only be stopped by force. We and France are today, in fulfilment of our obligation, going to the aid of Poland, who is so bravely resisting this wicked and unprovoked attack upon her people. We have a clear conscience. We have done all that any country could do to establish peace, but a situation in which no word given by Germany's ruler could be trusted and no people or country could feel themselves safe had become intolerable. And now that we have resolved to finish it, I know that you will all play your part with calmness and courage.

At such a moment as this the assurances of support that we have received from the Empire are a source of profound encouragement to us. Now may God bless you all and may he defend the right. For it is evil things that we shall be fighting against, brute force, bad faith, injustice, oppression and persecution. And against them I am certain that the right will prevail.

A newspaper seller's poster spreads the word. (IWM: HU 36171)

Neville Chamberlain announces the declaration of war to the nation.

Steel air-raid precaution shelters are delivered to a street in Muswell Hill, north London. (IWM: HU 36151)

Ellen Harris was a thirty-seven-year-old parliamentary reporter for Reuters News Agency, based in Fleet Street.

The first day I remember very well indeed, the announcement, 'This country is now at war,' and my saying – I was living in north London – to my husband, 'I shall have to get up to the office quickly, they'll be ringing but I'll get ready and go.'

He said, 'Well, I'll come with you, I can't allow you to go up there alone.'

Well, we got a bus and we'd gone two or three hundred yards, I suppose. And we got as far as Islington Green and the sirens went. And nobody knew – this was the first time ever. We'd had drill and training and what was impressed upon everybody was the gas mask. So now, here was the first warning, your mind immediately flew to the worst of everything. We were all turfed off the buses, people

On 23 August 1939 Nazi Germany and the Soviet Union had signed their non-aggression pact, which included a secret clause to partition Poland. On 25 August the Anglo-Polish Mutual Assistance Pact was signed. On 1 September 1939 the Nazis invaded Poland. The British government meanwhile hesitated over sending an ultimatum to Adolf Hitler until, under intense pressure from the House of Commons, in the late evening of 2 September 1939 it was sent. Hardly had the Prime Minister finished speaking when the sirens went off.

1 SEPTEMBER After softening-up air bombardments and supported by aircraft, German troops invade Poland

2 SEPTEMBER German troops and armour, supported by aircraft, advance across Poland; British cabinet sends Germany an ultimatum

didn't know what to expect, you see. Drivers, conductors, everybody, went down into a shelter. And this is where the driver stopped, right outside Islington Green shelter, which went right under the Green.

And as we all went in, mothers carrying little babies, even little babies with their gas masks on – immediately put on, you see – and the wardens were calling out 'Mind the live wires'. They hadn't finished the shelter. That to me was the first shock. I thought 'What a terrible thing, I wonder if this has happened all over the country.'

Well, we were there for a time and then it turned out to be a false alarm. They'd seen something off the coast and this alarm was given, put the wind up everybody but there was no raid. So that was my first introduction to wartime London.

Jean Mills was a seventeen-year-old, on vacation with her family on the east coast.

We were coming to the end of our holiday and we just heard the news on the Sunday morning. My father insisted on packing up immediately and rushing home. Of course we all thought that we were going to be bombed to bits straightaway from the word 'go', absolutely. We'd all been issued with gas masks and my father had had some kind of shelter built in our back garden and we were quite nervous I think because we just thought that the minute war was declared the Germans would be over and bombing us to bits. Of course it didn't really work out like that.

Mothers are instructed in the use of protective anti-gas helmets for children under two years old. (IWM: HU 33356)

3 SEPTEMBER Hitler ignores the ultimatum leading Britain and France to make an official declaration of war against Germany; Prime Minister Chamberlain informs the British people that 'a state of war now exists between Great Britain and Germany'

10 SEPTEMBER Headed by Field Marshal Gort, the first large units of the British Expeditionary Force embark for France

1939

CHAPTER TWO

FIRE AND WATER

WITHIN A WEEK OF NEVILLE CHAMBERLAIN'S declaration of war the first units of the British Expeditionary Force disembarked in France, and the rest of the British Commonwealth had declared war on Germany. In eastern Europe, by early October, the Poles had ceased fighting. By the end of the year units of the Indian Army had joined the BEF on the French and Belgian frontier, where, alongside its French allies, it sat, and waited. It was the 'phoney war'; it was not to last. On 8 April the Royal Navy mined Norwegian waters to prevent iron ore movement to Germany. On the 9th, the Germans launched a multi-pronged invasion of Norway – taking Denmark en route. In mid-April British ground forces landed in Norway, but, while the Royal Navy was to meet with success in its encounters with the German Navy, on 9 June, just a day after the British and French withdrew from the port of Narvik – the last of the Allied forces to leave Norway – the Norwegian army surrendered. Back in the House of Commons the debate on Norway on 7 and 8 May had found Chamberlain deserted by many of his own supporters. On 10 May Winston Churchill became Prime Minister; and on that same day the Germans invaded Holland and Belgium. On 15 May Holland capitulated.

The first contingent of British Expeditionary Forces to leave for France embark at Southampton. (IWM: H 27)

The Wehrmacht used massed tanks, the Luftwaffe provided aircraft – including terrifying Stuka dive-bombers, in a co-ordinated, mechanized attack. In the First World War the Allies had stood against the German armies on the Western Front for more than four years. In 1940 the German general, Heinz Guderian, from General Gerd von Rundstedt's Army Group A, took ten days to arrive on the French coast at Abbeville, on 20 May, and thus split the Allied forces in two. Six days later, the BEF's commander, Lord Gort was given the go-ahead for evacuation from France. The BEF and many other Allied units began to withdraw within a perimeter around Dunkirk. Outside it, on 23 May, von Rundstedt – on Hitler's authority – had ordered his armour to halt, leaving the Allied enclave to the attention of the Luftwaffe. The expectation in Britain was that, of the hundreds of thousands of British, Belgian, Canadian, Czechoslovak, and French soldiers, maybe 45,000 could be saved.

Across the English Channel, in Portsmouth,

Aided by overwhelming air support, German tanks make steady progress across the Netherlands.

Lord Gort, Commander-in-Chief of the British Expeditionary Forces. (IWM: H1)

German paratroopers land near Narvik during the invasion of Norway in April 1940.

Soldiers wait to be picked up from the waters off Dunkirk.
(IWM: HU 41240)

The roads to Dunkirk were clogged with refugees.
(IWM: HU 2284)

twenty-five-year-old **Elizabeth Quayle** of the Women's Auxiliary Air Force was on liaison duties, running the one phone line into Dunkirk. A few miles away a disaster was unfolding.

I'm rather ashamed to say it put the fear of God into me! Because every time you came on duty, we knew where the Huns were, we had maps with pins in, and they seemed to be advancing very fast. The Dunkirk crisis itself was unbelievable. It obviously built up. A lot of people coming back had jettisoned their guns and vehicles. They were pouring through. I think the officers at the other end of the phone were largely confined to their building, but they could see very clearly what was going on. It was absolute mayhem.

Dunkirk was full of people mostly who had walked, not in any form or order. They had just got there as fast as they could. Some had hitched lifts wherever possible. There were a lot of refugees coming in. It had been bombed. We knew that a lot

17 SEPTEMBER Soviet troops invade eastern Poland

29 SEPTEMBER Germany and the Soviet Union form a pact which leads to the partitioning of Poland

of the troops were sheltering in the buildings along the shore. We had no idea they were going to be rescued; it seemed the whole army was going to be bottled up there and the whole army was going to be captured.

Winston Churchill demanded that Sir Hugh Dowding, Commander-in-Chief of Fighter Command, commit more planes to the struggle in France against the Luftwaffe. It was a haphazard and costly operation, and Dowding feared that he would lose the ability to defend Great Britain given the losses that the RAF was incurring across the Channel. At Dunkirk the survival of armies that could, one day, fight again, was at stake. Hurricanes and Spitfires, flying from England, began the battle which was to continue over Britain, fighting above the beaches of Dunkirk. The

Tony Bartley was a Spitfire pilot with 92 Squadron during the evacuation at Dunkirk. (IWM: CNA 125)

troops meanwhile were subjected to continuous bombardment, and many felt that they had been let down by the RAF.

Tony Bartley, a pilot with 92 Squadron, was flying his Spitfire over Dunkirk.

There was a huge great thing of smoke and you saw all the troops going down to the beach. You saw a multitude of little craft. And there were naval ships shooting at everything, and lots of little boats came over. And the troops were just pouring down, going into the water, swimming out to the boats.

Nineteen-year-old **Hugh Dundas** of 616 (South Yorkshire) Squadron was then also a Spitfire pilot over Dunkirk:

There was this enormous great pall of smoke which was rising up from, I think, some oil tanks which had been set on fire, a huge black pillar of smoke that came up and spread out and then levelled off and went down the Channel for a distance of seventy-five to a hundred miles. Underneath that there was a lot of haze and general mayhem. It was altogether a very confusing scene, cloud, smoke.

13 NOVEMBER The first bombs to land on British soil are dropped on the Shetland Isles

17 DECEMBER Pocket battleship *Graf Spee* is scuttled in Montevideo harbour, having been trapped there by Royal Navy forces after the Battle of the River Plate

1939

I think that's one of the reasons why perhaps the Army had the impression that the Royal Air Force wasn't there half the time, because there was no control. We were outside the range of our own radar. We just had to go there. All the time one was playing a game of blind man's buff. Very often one wasn't at the right height. Of course the Germans were operating from fields which were comparatively close. They could come in and out very quickly. There was an awful lot of luck as to whether one was in the right place at the right time. Somebody looking back at it from an historical perspective who wasn't there imagines the coast of France, and Dunkirk, and a clear summer sky and lots of things on the beach and the sea and perhaps a little cloud here and there. It wasn't like that at all.

An illustration in the Italian newspaper *La Domenica del Corriere* depicts evacuating British forces under fire from the enemy.

Rescued troops watch burning stores from their ship.
(IWM: F 4868)

Operation Dynamo, the evacuation from Dunkirk, involved hundreds of vessels, from Royal Navy warships, through paddle-steamers to motorboats and yachts. One of the boats was the *Massey Shaw*, a shallow-draft firefighting ship based on the River Thames in London. Thirty-year-old **Francis Codd** of the Auxiliary Fire Brigade was a member of the crew.

We'd had lunch on a fine sunny day. And suddenly the bell went, to assemble us all. So we trooped out – all of the auxiliaries on duty at that time at Blackfriars; I suppose there were about seventy or eighty of us – assembled in the usual place, which was on the staircase and landing at Blackfriars. And the station officer – looking very solemn and backed by his lieutenants – said, 'A message from Lambeth

I JANUARY Two million 19–27-year-olds in Britain are called up to join the war effort

16 MARCH The first British civilian is killed during an attack by fifteen Junkers Ju 88 bombers on the Grand Fleet's anchorage in Scapa Flow

Headquarters. The Massey Shaw is going to Dunkirk.' 'Oh,' everyone gasped. We'd no idea what would be the duties of the Massey Shaw. We imagined of course that it would be fighting fires. And someone suggested the whole sea would a sheet of flame and we'd have to guide the Massey Shaw through acres of flaming sea, carving away with our monitor to get to ships or people or whatever we might be required to do.

So with that awful vision the station officer said, 'Now, I want a crew which will be under the skipper of the Massey Shaw with the engine crew of regulars. And I want about half a dozen auxiliary volunteers.' There was a tiny second of hesitation. And then as one man we all stepped forward and held our hands up and that threw the station officer into complete confusion. He didn't know what to do because he'd got to choose about six out of about seventy people. So there was a lot of debate. And they decided that they would choose the senior enrolled people as our main priority. So as my name was in fact the earliest of the whole station I had a right under this direction to be one of the crew, which I eagerly held as my right to be one of the volunteers ...

We left Ramsgate in the afternoon. The sea was like a millpond. Quite exceptional. The whole weather had been, right through May, continuous sunshine and no storm, no wind. It was perfect weather. In fact the sea was as warm as it would be in midsummer, because we got to know about that when we got to Dunkirk and had to stand in the sea and spend all night wet through and felt no cold. We started off. And there was the horizon and no coast visible, until after an hour or so the first thing we could see was a black column of smoke, visible perhaps from ten miles away. And as we got nearer and nearer this seemed to be more menacing. It became an enormous black menace. We thought perhaps the whole of Dunkirk was alight and burning. As we got closer we could see that it was an oil fire. Some of the oil installations

Firefighting barges on the Thames attempt to douse the flames from a burning building.

had been ignited and it was burning – as they do – with black smoke, probably go on for a day or two. Then we could see the outline of the coast, flat, no distinguishing marks. And then from about a mile away, still no aeroplanes, no bombs, no menace; then we could see it was a flat beach, a sandy beach, and then we saw the silhouette of houses against this sky, the setting sun; not a continuous line of buildings but breaks in the buildings and what could be a hotel and then a house and then another hotel, then several houses. We could see that silhouette.

We couldn't see what was on the beach. We gradually saw reflections on the calm water. And I thought I could see a wrecked small craft and then

9 APRIL The German invasion of Norway begins with the occupation of major Norwegian ports by advance detachments of German troops

Simultaneously, German troopships, covered by aircraft, are sent into Copenhagen harbour as Denmark becomes occupied territory

1940

*a bigger craft. Gradually we could see dark shapes
against the sand. And then we saw that there were
hundreds, thousands, of people on this sand and
stretching up to the line of houses which stood
presumably on the road that ran along the coast.*

*It was an extraordinary sight. Nothing seemed to
be happening. They didn't seem to be moving in any
organized way, not marching. They were standing or
sitting. But mainly we noticed that they were columns
of men stretching down to the sea and into the sea.
We didn't really understand what this was at first.
And then it suddenly occurred to us that these were
columns of men waiting to be picked up, lined up
ready, that the first man in the sea was the next man
to be picked up.*

*So we came in slowly in our craft, watching
everything, not knowing quite what we were supposed
to do. But we knew we would have no instructions.
We'd have to make our own plans. The skipper of the
Massey Shaw was quite rightly very apprehensive that
the props – because there were two engines – would
get tangled up with the lines and debris that was in
the water nearer the shore. Although we had a very
shallow draft it seemed to be a high risk. In fact the
props did get jammed. And we had to jump out of the
boat, switch off the engines of course, free the*

*propeller from tangled rope. So we decided it would be
fatal to go too far in. Although we could have gone in
to probably three or four feet of water, we stayed in
about six feet of water some fifty yards further back
than we could have been because it was a shallow
sea. And we didn't know what the tide was doing at
that moment. And we thought we'd drop anchor,
which we did. We then realized that we'd get a line
ashore. What were we to fix it to?*

*Well, one of our auxiliaries, Shiner Wright, was a
good swimmer. And he went from the Massey Shaw
some fifty to a hundred yards to a wrecked boat which
was right inshore in about two or three feet of water.
He swam with what we called the 'grass line', which is
a rope that floats on water. And he tied it to the wreck
so that we had a fixed line into shallow water.*

*Now, there were lots of little rowing boats in the
water, mainly sunk or not being used. So they got a
rowing boat that would hold very few people, a light
rowing boat, and worked it along the line pulling hand
over hand. When we got organized this worked very
well. Whoever was in charge of the column of men
lined up near the shore end of the line detailed six
men into the rowing boat to pull along the line till they
reached the Massey Shaw, climb out on board and
send their rowing boat back for another half dozen.*

10 MAY Winston Churchill becomes British Prime
Minister, following the resignation of Neville
Chamberlain after the débâcle of the Allied

intervention in Norway; he forms a war cabinet
comprising members from the main political parties;
the German invasion of Holland and Belgium begins

And this went on – a bit of a slow process, but it was the only way. And there didn't seem to be any real urgency. It was still another hour or two of daylight. And in that way we got, I think we took aboard thirty-six soldiers out of the water that night. And when we were full there was nothing more we could do. We upped anchor and set course for Ramsgate.

The Dunkirk evacuation ended on 4 June 1940. Some 224,585 British Commonwealth and 112,546 French and Belgian soldiers had been rescued. By late June more than half a million men, in total, had been evacuated from France.

Soon after the last Allied troops had left Dunkirk two young Luftwaffe members arrived. They were friends, anti-Nazis and deeply depressed by Hitler's triumph. One of them was **Bernt Engelman**.

On the beaches and in the dunes north of Dunkirk thousands of light and heavy weapons lay in the sands, along with munitions crates, field kitchens, scattered cans of rations and innumerable wrecks of British army trucks.

'Damn!' I exclaimed to Erwin. 'The entire British army went under here!'

Erwin should his head vigorously. 'On the

contrary! A miracle took place here! If the German tanks and Stukas and navy had managed to surround the British here, shooting most of them, and taking the rest prisoner, then England wouldn't have any trained soldiers left. Instead the British seem to have rescued them all – and a lot of Frenchmen too. Adolf can say goodbye to his blitzkrieg against England . . . '

On 22 June France surrendered. **Elizabeth Quayle**, from her job in French Liaison heard the news early:

I was extremely upset, because it never occurred to me that we would survive. I thought we were defeated, and frankly thought we would surrender and sue for peace.

Nineteen-year-old **Roland Beamont** had flown a Hurricane with 87 Squadron in France and Belgium.

We who'd been in the French battle came home convinced that there was only one thing that was going to stop the enemy crossing the Channel and that would be us. We could see that coming all the way through the summer. By July and August it was building up to a fury. We knew absolutely that there was just one front line holding. It had to be us that did it.

The evacuation process is long and arduous, with thousands of troops awaiting transportation. (IWM: NYP 68075)

12 MAY German forces cross the Franco-Belgian frontier and begin their advance across France

14 MAY Lord Beaverbrook appointed Minister for Aircraft production; Dutch forces cease resistance against Germany, after the initial invasion on May 10

1940

CHAPTER THREE

SEALION

On 4 June 1940 the sixty-five-year-old Prime Minister, Winston Churchill, addressed the House of Commons.

Even though large tracts of Europe and many old and famous States have fallen or may fall into the grip of the Gestapo and all the odious apparatus of Nazi rule, we shall not flag or fail. We shall go on to the end, we shall fight in France, we shall fight on the seas and oceans, we shall fight with growing confidence and growing strength in the air, we shall defend our Island, whatever the cost may be, we shall fight on the beaches, we shall fight on the

Winston Churchill makes one of numerous radio broadcasts to the British nation.

landing grounds, we shall fight in the fields and in the streets, we shall fight in the hills; we shall never surrender, and even if, which I do not for a moment believe, this Island or a large part of it were subjugated and starving, then our Empire beyond the seas, armed and guarded by the British Fleet, would carry on the struggle, until, in God's good time, the New World, with all its power and might, steps forth to the rescue and the liberation of the old.

Refugees from across Europe had arrived in Britain, and many German anti-Nazis were promptly interned on the Isle of Man. One of them was **Dr Klaus Hinrichsen**.

A poster reminds citizens of the need to stand united against the enemy in wartime.
(IWM: PST 0069)

Schoolboys up and down the country make a valuable contribution to the war effort by felling trees.
(IWM: FX 8212D)

"The South Downs"

your BRITAIN · *fight for it now*

ISSUED BY A·B·C·A

Highway authorities begin a campaign to remove signposts in order to confuse the enemy in the event of invasion. (IWM: HU 49250)

Once Dunkirk was over and it was a question of only defending Britain I think one thought, 'It will take a long time but Britain will win.' Otherwise you could only commit suicide.

In June 1940, the family of **Hugh Dundas** was living in Yorkshire.

Even there, far away from the Channel, there were constant preparations taking place then. People cutting down trees and putting them in fields and taking all the signs down in the little by-roads, and all roads. There was a real feeling in the country that invasion was likely. After all, we'd seen what had happened in Poland and France and Holland and Belgium. There wasn't much doubt about what we were up to in anybody's mind.

At the end of May 1940 a debate took place within the British cabinet on which the future of the world turned. Lord Halifax urged his colleagues to consider the possibility of a negotiated peace with Hitler. It was a reasonable position. France was about to fall to Germany, the rest of the continent had gone, or was going the same way. Hitler had expressed his admiration for the British Empire; there was the possibility that Britain would be allowed to keep that, while returning German's colonies – taken away in 1918 – and allowing Germany a free hand in Eastern Europe. To fight on seemed – unreasonable. Churchill, backed by Chamberlain, rejected Halifax's proposal.

In Berlin it seemed likely to the Nazis that the British would make a deal, the Germans had clearly won the war. But moves had meanwhile begun for an invasion, and early in July Hitler ordered his armed forces to step up the planning. The Luftwaffe commander Hermann Göring said it would take just four days to knock out the RAF in southern England, an essential prelude to

15 MAY Oil and transport targets in the Ruhr are bombed by ninety-nine RAF aircraft, marking the start of the strategic bombing offensive; Air Marshal Dowding, commanding Fighter Command, is put under pressure to send more fighter aircraft to France but he resists, arguing that their presence is essential to the fundamental defence of Britain

Churchill's coalition War Cabinet, formed in May 1940.
(IWM: HU 55505)

Lord Halifax (left), whose wish to negotiate peace with Hitler was rejected by Churchill.
(IWM: HU 5539 FL)

invasion. But the Nazi dictator was still uncertain. On 16 July came the order for Operation Sealion, the invasion of Britain. On 19 July came Hitler's 'Last Appeal To Reason' speech, broadcast worldwide, ignored in Britain.

The situation seemed desperate. In less than a decade Fascist air power had made Abyssinia, Nanking, and Guernica synonyms for terror. On 14 May Rotterdam had joined the list; a Luftwaffe raid on the city killed 980 people and injured 29,000. Yet the British government had several cards up its sleeve. Between 1929 and 1945 **Frederick**

26 MAY The order is given for the start of Operation Dynamo, the evacuation of the British Expeditionary Force and of French troops from the port and beaches at Dunkirk

27 MAY The most diverse selection of vessels gathers in ports along the English Channel coastline, ranging from tugs and ferries, pleasure boats, fishing boats and Thames cabin cruisers

Winterbotham served with the Air Staff Department, Secret Intelligence Service. In Germany in the 1930s he met Hitler, and Albert Kesselring who was to command the Luftwaffe's Luftflotte 2 (Air Fleet 2) in the Battle of Britain.

Throughout the war, from Bletchley Park, Winterbotham supervised the organization and distribution of 'Ultra' material – top secret German communications – to senior

Field Marshal Albert Kesselring, commander of the Luftwaffe's Luftflotte 2.
(IWM: HU 5140)

Seconds after falling from a Junker 52: German troops parachute into Holland.
(IWM: GER 295W)

A poster promoting the Luftwaffe, air force of the Third Reich.

1940

28 MAY Belgium capitulates, surrendering to the Nazis

31 MAY Sir Oswald Mosley, founder and leader of the British Union of Fascists, is interned under defence regulations; released 1943

4 JUNE Completion of Operation Dynamo, the evacuation of Dunkirk, which saw the rescue of more than 337,000 Allied troops, two-thirds of them British; Churchill makes his rousing 'We shall fight them on the beaches…' speech

10 JUNE Italy declares war on the Allies; Germany completes its occupation of Norway

commanders and the Prime Minister. The British – partly following earlier Polish efforts – had cracked the German encoding machine, and Ultra, which expanded throughout the war, was the fruit of that success.

The Luftwaffe started getting on the air and at this time we knew, more or less, what the strength of the Luftwaffe was. But we didn't know exactly how they were going to be placed, but we got the positions from Ultra of all the Luftwaffe – all their units, wherever they happened to be, and the air fleets, with old Kesselring in command of one of them. And so we

had the whole line-up of the German Air Force easily planned before they started. Some of them were still up in Holland, and others stretched right down to Brittany, and the functions of each of their squadrons became quite obvious because the whole of the rearrangement came through on the air.

This was the beginning of Sealion. It wasn't until the actual Battle of Britain had started that we got the

German parachute troops fill the Dutch skies in May 1940. (IWM: HU 4590)

11 JUNE French government leaves Paris for Tours; at the new HQ, Churchill meets the French cabinet, but refuses to send RAF fighter squadrons to France, believing that Britain's defences would be compromised as a result

14 JUNE German troops enter Paris

German parachute troops go into action following a safe landing on Dutch soil. (IWM: MH 8059)

orders from Göring through to his squadrons that now they were going to conquer Britain and that the Führer had given permission and that Operation Sealion would be undertaken, so we had something to go on then. And we started getting all the movements of the German troops up to the coast and we got the installation in Holland of a number of what they called air loading points, where an aeroplane could come in, and rather like railway platforms, there would be two platforms either side of it, so that it could be reloaded with troops or equipment in a matter of minutes, and then turned round and off again. And the invasion was obviously to be on these lines, parachutes dropped and an immense amount of equipment dropped by air, and all the time the German Air Force would be bombing behind, and fighter squadrons – the whole plan of the invasion was there.

16 JUNE As German forces advance through France Marshal Pétain, recently appointed head of the French government, proposes an armistice to Germany

17 JUNE Churchill delivers his 'Finest Hour' speech

18 JUNE From London, Brigadier-General Charles de Gaulle broadcasts to the French people, urging them to fight on; the RAF bombs Hamburg and Bremen

1940

CHAPTER FOUR

A BUNCH OF CHAPS

THE GERMAN ADVANCE HAD BEEN GREATLY assisted by the Wehrmacht's use of paratroopers. In May 1940, as the Regular army was fighting its way out of France, the British set up what was originally called the Local Defence Volunteers, which by July had become the Home Guard. Its tasks were to man roadblocks, watch out for those ubiquitous paratroopers and carry out acts of sabotage to delay the invaders.

As the threat of invasion grew, people like forty-five-year-old **Harold Gower**, a First World War veteran, became the backbone of the new organization. He was a musketry-training officer in Amersham and London from 1940 to 1945 for the Home Guard, assessing its new recruits.

Except for a few in Amersham, in the villages they were just a bunch of chaps – that's all. They didn't know a damn thing, really. Although some of them had been in the forces before they didn't seem to me to know anything. I don't think they knew which end of a gun the bullet came out of, really. They took a helluva lot of training. They were a mixture of ages, reserved occupations most of them, that is to say they were farm labourers or whatever. We didn't have plans for blowing up bridges because we had no explosives of any sort. Only Molotov cocktails and that sort of thing.

Wartime painting of a member of the Lancashire Home Guard.

One of the duties of the Home Guard was to man roadblocks, to ensure that roads were properly barricaded in the event of invasion. (IWM: HU 65877)

A member of the Local Defence Volunteers (LDV), forerunner of the Home Guards, engages in rifle practice.

John Graham went on to fight in Normandy and ended up a Major-General, but in 1940 he was just seventeen years old, and he joined his local Home Guard.

> It was the Isle of Wight battalion. The battalion commander was a General Oglander-Aspinall, who I think had been Hamilton's Chief of Staff in the Dardanelles in the First World War. My company commander was Sir Ralph Gore, who lived at Bembridge, who was a great yachtsman. My platoon

Members of the Home Guard prepare for a camouflage exercise.

> commander was Tom Love, who became the local publican. And they made me a lance-corporal although I was the youngest member, on the strength of having got certificate A in the Cheltenham College Officer Training Unit. And we spent some very happy months there. We had American P14 rifles, fifty rounds of ammunition, a civilian gas mask, a leather

22 JUNE France capitulates and signs an armistice with Germany

28 JUNE Great Britain officially recognizes de Gaulle as leader of the Free French

belt, leather gaiters, boots and a bayonet. We went on duty as a section every fifth night for which we got one and threepence to cover the cost of the sandwiches. I've said I was the youngest member of the platoon. The oldest chap, Chichester – sergeant – had been in the Boer War. He was the best shot of the lot of us. The others varied in age between about sixty-plus to me, aged, I think, just seventeen.

On a village green in Surrey, two Home Guardsmen practice using a Vickers machine gun in December 1940. (IWM: H 5842)

And as far as I remember the section consisted of a chap called Smith – a gentleman of leisure who'd only got one arm – he'd lost the other one in the First World War – and a chap called Allen, the local electrician who was therefore in a reserved occupation, and couldn't become a full-time serviceman, Henley the baker's boy, who had TB, and my particular colleague with whom I always did stag – went on sentry duty – was Mick Curran. And Mick Curran had been a stoker at the Battle of Jutland in the Royal Navy – and a most amusing colleague but he suffered terribly from wind. And we used to go on duty together – used to do stag – in a field of cows

30 JUNE German forces land in the Channel Islands, the only enemy occupation of the British Isles during the war, which lasts until 1945; during June Allied ships fare badly against German U-boats, losing more than 350,000 tons

2 JULY First daylight raid against Britain by German bombers

1940

behind Nodes Fort. Nodes Fort is in the Isle of Wight not very far from Ryde, pointing in the general direction of Portsmouth and Southsea. And of course from our vantage point we could see Portsmouth and Southampton, and even London on a clear night, being bombed, as it was very heavily during all this period. But with the noise of the bombing and Mick Curran's wind we didn't get a great deal of sleep.

Just back from rescuing soldiers on the *Massey Shaw* at Dunkirk, **Francis Codd** encountered the Home Guard:

I looked a bit extraordinary. I remember I was wearing the reefer jacket of the auxiliary fireman and the dark trousers. I had an open neck white tennis shirt and my cap. That was all I had. And I'd got white plimsolls. Now I was extremely sunburnt.

And my hair being fair always bleaches completely, almost white, and was a bit long and unruly. When I got to Sandwich on my way back to Ramsgate – Sandwich is a place I've known since a child and has always been one of my favourite towns – and I thought, well, I must have a walk round in the hour I'd got to wait between buses, walk round the town and have a look at the churches. And there was one big churchyard. I'm not sure it isn't called St Clement's and a particularly fine church. So I walked towards it. And stood in the churchyard looking up at the tower, the old flint tower, and admiring it on this calm beautiful summer evening,

A Home Guard squad learns bayonet fighting techniques as part of its overall training.

38

10 JULY The Luftwaffe bombs military targets in southern England to test the response of the RAF, which signals the start of the Battle of Britain;

Germany views the air battles as a precursor to possible invasion, whereas Britain sees it as a last stand against conquest and subjugation

A Home Guardsman practises using a Tommy gun during a training session at the War Office School in Surrey.

and suddenly I was pounced on by two enormous men. And I didn't know what had happened. And they didn't seem to be hurting me. But their obvious enmity towards me was a bit offputting. And they were feeling for guns. Anyway they frisked me, the only time I think in my life I have ever been frisked. And they looked in my pockets for something incriminating. Nothing really that I can remember I'd got with me.

They said, 'We've had a lot of German spies here, you know. And we're not satisfied.'

So I said, 'Well, I'm not a German spy.'

They said, 'Well, we think you might be. You look German.'

13 JULY Hitler declares that Germany's air offensive will commence on 5 August

16 JULY Hitler sets out his plans for Operation Sealion – the invasion of England – in his Directive 16, but does not reveal a target date

1940

So I said, 'I don't.' I said, 'This is my standard uniform. I've been to Dunkirk.'

They said, 'Well, that's your story.'

I argued and remonstrated with them for some time. I said, 'I've got a bus to catch.'

They said, 'Come along to the police station.'

Well, that was the first I'd heard of the Home Guard in action. And they were just enthusiastic local Sandwich Home Guard people, thought they had trapped a German descended on them by parachute and out to take all sorts of notes about church towers and points of advantage for troops

due to arrive just after me. I could see the comic side. And of course I didn't really treat it seriously. I knew they would get nowhere. Anyway: 'Well, we'd better ring up London and check that you come from London and that you are a fireman.'

Well, they set about it in such a hopeless way, ringing London headquarters of the Fire Brigade and unwilling to disclose my name in case it was a

Using a sunken railway track as a trench, members of the Home Guard practise throwing hand grenades.

40

19 JULY Addressing the Reichstag, Hitler issues what he describes as a 'final appeal to common sense' to Great Britain

23 JULY The Local Defence Volunteers, raised as an auxiliary force to combat a German invasion, are renamed as the Home Guard

Home Guardsmen in Battalion Areas are trained to use light anti-aircraft guns for use against low-flying daylight raiders. A Battalion Home Guard gun team from Devon is in action in March 1944.

(IWM: HU 42535)

pseudonym. And it was two hours before I was driven back by the police in a police car in state, back to our headquarters in Ramsgate. Rumour of course had reached them by then from London because they'd been alerted by then that Codd of the River Service had been arrested in Ramsgate for spying.

The Home Guard were not discouraged by their misplaced zeal. **John Graham**:

I think we were rather proud of ourselves. It also was time that somebody in khaki did rather better than the BEF had done in France and what our allies had done of course hitherto. Although we had minimal equipment and very little training and were pretty senile or juvenile, we had a good spirit and it was our territory. We felt the Germans if they came would be at a disadvantage initially, I mean either seasick or parachuted or something. We did at least know the fields and the hedges and everything else. And we'd put up a good show for about half a day. And that would be the end of us. But they never came.

31 JULY Since May 1940 1,200 fighter aircraft have been produced in Britain, substantially closing the gap between the relative strengths of the RAF and the Luftwaffe

1 AUGUST Hitler updates his plan for the invasion of England in Directive 17, with a target date of 19-26 September; he orders the 'destruction of the RAF and the British aircraft industry'

1940

CHAPTER FIVE

MACHINES, MORALE AND MISSILES

THE AIR WAR OVER BRITAIN IN 1940 WAS TO BE different from any encounter the Luftwaffe had faced. The RAF was flying over its homeland. German fighters were flying at the limit of their range. It was a conflict between two major industrial powers, and for the first time the Germans did not have the technological upper hand. Two fighter aircraft came to symbolize British hopes of survival. The Supermarine Spitfire, and the Hawker Hurricane, powered by an engine with a name resonant of Arthurian myth, the Rolls-Royce Merlin. In the mid-1930s, from the Air Ministry, **Frederick Winterbotham** had watched with fascination the development of one of Britain's new weapons.

Designed by R. J. Mitchell, the Supermarine Spitfire first entered active service in 1938, and was one of the fastest and most effective single-seat fighters of the Second World War.

The Spitfire had been designed by this man down in Southampton [R. J. Mitchell] who had been designing the Schneider Trophy aeroplanes before. He had really studied the flight of birds – he was a very brilliant man. I so well remember when the Air Staff were asked down to see the test flight of the first Spitfire, and some of my friends from the Air Ministry went down, and they were so excited about this aeroplane. All through the Air Ministry it was terribly secret. Nobody had to know anything about it, but it really looked as if we were going to have something which would match up to anything that the Germans could build.

The Spitfire first entered service in August 1938. The Hurricane had entered service in 1937. **Roland Beamont** flew it from 1939.

I particularly wanted to fly the Hurricane because I was impressed with it. I'm not quite sure why. I think the Spitfire always looked like a beautiful and

The Hawker Hurricane – the first RAF plane to exceed a speed of 300 miles an hour in level flight – was crucial to the victory over the Luftwaffe in the Battle of Britain. (IWM: CM 2116)

elegant aeroplane but I felt that the Hurricane was somehow more rugged. Anyway it attracted me very much. I was delighted when I got on to it.

Hugh Dundas flew the Spitfire.

It was a lovely aeroplane to fly. The only thing was at that stage that we still had canvas or fabric ailerons. It wasn't until the beginning of 1941 that we got metal ailerons, which made a tremendous difference to the handling of the Spitfires at the high speed of a dive. With the canvas ailerons it became very, very heavy laterally, but with the metal ailerons there was a tremendous difference. They had certain other shortcomings from an operational

point of view. For instance, when we went to Dunkirk we didn't have self-sealing petrol tanks. Of course the petrol tanks in the Spitfire were just in front of one's feet. We didn't have rear-view mirrors. One of the first things we did after our first one or two engagements at Dunkirk was to go down to the local motor agency and get rear-view mirrors and have them screwed on to the top of our windscreens.

Roland Beamont:

In 1940 the Spitfire was what it still is today, probably the most elegant and beautiful single-seater fighter aeroplane that's ever been built. And it was very delicate and nice to fly. The Hurricane was more rugged, rather more pugnacious-looking, equally pleasant to fly – in fact in many ways nicer to fly

Spitfire pilot, Wing Commander Hugh Dundas DFC., AAF, who later achieved major success during the invasions of Sicily and Italy. (IWM: CH 4545)

Wing Commander Roland Beamont, DSO., DFC., successful, courageous pilot of the Hawker Hurricane. (IWM: CL 1389)

1940

8 AUGUST A senior British Secret Intelligence officer, Wing Commander F. W. Winterbotham, alerts Air Marshal Dowding, upon discovery of Göring's orders for the air offensive against England

10 AUGUST Adlertag ('Eagle Day') – the date on which Göring's air offensive was due to commence – is postponed for three days due to bad weather

because it was rather more stable. The Spitfire was agile, and because of this a slightly more – it's rather difficult to describe it – delicate aeroplane. It certainly had a very delicate undercarriage. You could very easily break the undercarriage by landing it across wind or hitting bumps. And a lot of Spitfire losses throughout the war years were caused by undercarriage failure. The Hurricane, by contrast, had a big, broad, strong undercarriage, which would iron out the bumps and also iron out pilot inaccuracies. It had a very good record on landing. The Hurricane was a better gun platform; you could aim the guns more accurately than you could with a Spitfire. Again, because it was better directionally than the Spitfire, which was always a little bit wandery.

The basic plan on all the big intercepts was that the Hurricanes were vectored against the bomber streams, and the Spitfires were held in reserve, or not necessarily held in reserve, but were directed immediately to the higher altitudes to intercept the escorting fighters.

And then there were the Germans.

In 1940 twenty-one-year-old **Tony Bartley** was flying a Spitfire with 92 Squadron.

The Spitfire was probably the finest combat aircraft. The Germans had the Messerschmitt Bf 109 and they had other things ... they had [later, in 1941] the Focke-Wulf 190, which was a desperately good aeroplane. But the Spitfire started with a 1200-horsepower Rolls-Royce Merlin engine, which was a marvellous engine, and the final one in the same airframe was 2400 horsepower. The Focke-Wulf in 1942 was a better aeroplane than a Mark V Spitfire. And the 109e was better than a Mark V. But finally

Spitfire formation. The earliest version of the Spitfire had a top speed of about 360 miles (580 km) per hour and an armament of eight .303-inch machine guns. (IWM: HU 5637)

12 AUGUST Radar stations along the Kent, Sussex and Isle of Wight coasts are raided by Messerschmitt Bf 110s and Junkers Ju 87 Stukas

13 AUGUST Following a brief delay caused by bad weather, the first major action of the Battle of Britain takes place

1940

the Spitfire, with only adding a small bit on the frame, I think it was about another nine or ten inches or something, encompassed twice the horsepower. And it was the best aeroplane.

The Messerschmitt Bf 109 was the Luftwaffe's premier fighter, faster at climbing or diving than the Spitfire or Hurricane, but less manouevrable. (IWM: HU 2742)

Roland Beamont:

We had been told in aircraft recognition classes of the various characteristics of the Heinkel 111, the Dornier 17, the Messerschmitt 109, which were the three main aeroplanes we might meet, and also the Ju 87 Stuka. Later on we heard more about the Ju 88, which was a very much higher performance dive bomber, medium twin-engined bomber. In all that I don't think we ever heard that the German aircraft, our opposition, had anything that was superior to ours. The way the affairs of Fighter Command were carried on there was always present the tacit assumption that you had better equipment and were better trained and were altogether a more capable chap than the opposition were going to be. There wasn't any foreboding about it, one didn't feel

scared of the enemy. It's odd this, because we had every right to be scared of them, particularly the experienced ones from the Spanish war. There was no tendency towards a feeling of inferiority in personnel or equipment. I think we had a respect for the Messerschmitt 109. We thought it was probably a very capable aeroplane but we didn't think there was any reason why it should be more capable than our Hurricanes.

Fliers from Britain, New Zealand, Poland, the Irish Republic, Belgium, Canada, Jamaica, Czechoslovakia, the future Israel, the United States, Australia, France, Newfoundland, South Africa, Southern Rhodesia (Zimbabwe) and Poland took part in the battle.

14 AUGUST In spite of more bad weather, the RAF flies 700 sorties and downs 45 Luftwaffe aircraft

15 AUGUST The Luftwaffe deploys in force with more than 2,000 sorties over England; RAF Fighter Command responds by deploying all three of its Groups for the first time

The Focke-Wulf 190 was a single-seat fighter that went into service in 1941 to supplement the Me 109. It was described as Germany's best piston-engined fighter.
(IWM: MH 4190)

In May 1940 a newspaper illustration depicts Ju 87 Stukas dive-bombing Norwegian railway installations to hamper resistance to the German invasion.

Tony Bartley:

If one had a slight weakness in some area, then somebody from Australia or New Zealand, or something, then compensated for it, and the whole conglomerate, the whole team together, the Commonwealth, mostly Commonwealth. We had Czechs and Poles who were very brave and we had a Frenchman in our squadron who joined the Battle of Britain. Together it made an absolutely indestructible team because the morale, everybody's

16 AUGUST Military sites in southern and south-eastern England are targeted by the Luftwaffe during 1,700 sorties, while the RAF bombers attack the Fiat manufacturing plant in Turin

18 AUGUST The first Luftwaffe aircraft is brought down over London; German bombers successfully hit and damage Kenley and Tangmere RAF stations as well as other Surrey and Kent airfields

1940

Spitfire pilots relax and play cards in between missions. (IWM: CH 1759)

morale, was compensated by the others. And the whole thing, put together, was undefeatable because the spirit was – we never thought we could – nobody ever said, what happens if we lose the Battle of Britain? None of us ever thought, it never even crossed our minds that we would lose. That mélange of different nationalities that made up the fighter pilots: I always had the feeling it contributed a great deal to the overall fortitude and confidence.

Roland Beamont:

One of the things that won the Battle of Britain was the morale of the squadrons. That wasn't a thing that happened by itself. It was created by the leaders in the air force. It was enhanced and kept going by the squadron and flight commanders. The squadron commanders were in their late twenties, the flight commanders were in their early twenties – they were all boys. They were a very remarkable group of people who didn't allow the situation to appear to be anything of any great importance.

As the Blitz ebbed in 1941, the Royal Air Force's bombing of Germany was to grow in

20 AUGUST Churchill broadcasts his inspirational tribute to the RAF pilots fighting the Battle of Britain: 'Never in the field of human conflict was so much owed by so many to so few'

24 AUGUST Several civilians are killed when a German bomber veers off course and offloads over central London

intensity. By 1942 vast raids were beginning to devastate that country's cities. But in June 1944 the first unmanned V-1 flying bombs, each carrying almost a ton of explosive, began landing in England. The pulse-jet-powered V-1 'vengeance weapon' anticipated cruise missiles – although no one would have used such a term. Later that year the V-1 was joined by the V-2 rocket. It was the world's first missile blitz, an augury of a chilling future, and of the race to the moon of the 1960s. The future was born then.

Roland Beamont, by then twenty-four, commanded an RAF fighter wing which shot down V-1s over southern England in 1944.

They looked like a very small slim single-seater fighter aeroplane, cigar-shaped fuselage, little thin wings and a big jet pipe at the back. It was the first jet aeroplane I'd ever seen.

Aircrew check their flying kit before being driven to their dispersal areas. (IWM: D 6022)

25 AUGUST In retaliation for the raid on London, RAF bombers launch an attack on Berlin. Earlier in the year Reichsmarschall Hermann Göring, head of the Luftwaffe, had declared in a broadcast: 'If a single British bomb falls on Berlin, you may call me "Mayer".' On the morning after the RAF's visit, the name Mayer is seen scrawled on buildings and vehicles all over Berlin

CHAPTER SIX

EYES AND EARS

BEFORE THE SECOND WORLD WAR THE IDEA THAT 'the bomber will always get through' had become widely accepted. Experiences like the destruction in 1937 of Guernica during the Spanish civil war seemed to confirm it. The scientist Robert Watson-Watt disagreed. On 12 February 1935, in an experiment using a BBC transmitter at Daventry, he employed radio energy to detect an approaching RAF bomber. In 1936 he became head of the new Bawdsey research station near Felixstowe to explore the use of 'Radio Direction Finding' (RDF), as radar was misleadingly labelled. By 1938 a coastal chain of radar stations was under construction. By 1940 a system, in advance of anything in the world, was operational.

Roland Beamont:

The RDF that had been established, with brilliant foresight, just before the war did provide – in the area roughly from I suppose Portland Bill round to the north of the Thames estuary – something like 100 to 120 miles' warning of aircraft flying into our air space at altitudes above 15,000 feet. This gave sufficient warning of the formation and the progress of any enemy bomber raids to be given to our fighter squadrons to get them up into position to intercept, rather than flying wildly round the sky hoping to meet up with something. We did win; the Germans knew they lost. The fact that we had radar was probably the key to enabling us to win.

From the twenty-one 'Chain Home' radar stations, information on approaching enemy aircraft was sent to Fighter Command Headquarters at Bentley Priory in Stanmore, then to the four Fighter Group HQs covering England and from there to individual fighter bases. But in 1940 the RAF had a severe shortage of manpower, mechanics, fitters, construction workers – and staff to operate

SERVE IN THE WAAF
WITH THE MEN WHO FLY

Scientist Robert Watson-Watt, who was responsible for the development of radar, which led to the construction of a coastal chain of radar stations.
(IWM: CH 13862)

Poster advertising recruitment to the Women's Auxiliary Air Force (WAAF).
(IWM: PST 3096)

the new radar system and the control rooms. So the authorities, despite initial resistance, opted for womanpower. Recruits to the Women's Auxiliary Air Force (WAAF) began to supplement, and then replace men.

Twenty-one-year-old **Diana Pitt Parsons** had been studying art before the war. By 1940 she was training as a radar operator.

You have a transmitter station, which sends out a signal which hits the aircraft and the signal comes back to the reception area, and you have a means of calibrating the distance, finding the distance in between, which you then display on a display unit. So you can judge how far away the aeroplane is and

Examples of the aerials used by Chain Home Low Stations to detect low-flying aircraft approaching the British coastline.
(IWM: CH 15183 & IWM: CH 15173)

1940

27 AUGUST The Luftwaffe carries out night raids on 21 British cities

31 AUGUST Over a two-week period the RAF and Luftwaffe suffer combined losses of over 800 aircraft, the latter losing 467 fighters and bombers, and many more airmen than the RAF, as far more German aircrew are taken prisoner

you have, in those days, a pretty rough idea of its height and its azimuthal position. If you picked an aeroplane up at a very far range, you knew it must be pretty high because of the way the radio waves – what they called the polar diagram – went out, which meant that it must be high or you wouldn't be seeing it, because the waves go upwards, because of the curvature of the earth. They go straight out. So that was the sort of thing we worked on to begin with. It was a complicated business.

A lot of the girls in radar had been to boarding schools. They chose those girls of that background. And I always insist that, after a girls' boarding school,

anything'd be quite blissful. I mean, being in the WAAF was freedom after knowing what a girls' school could be like.

Anne Duncan, who was twenty-three at the time, trained as a plotter in Leighton Buzzard.

It was three weeks' training as far as I remember. We were billeted in a beautiful country house and taken by bus each day. The first day I remember going into it we were absolutely fascinated because it was all covered in netting with camouflage over the top. We couldn't think why, but we realized then

4 SEPTEMBER Hitler declares his intention to reduce London to rubble, and to raze other British cities to the ground, in response to RAF attacks on Germany

5 SEPTEMBER Responding to Hitler's pledge the Luftwaffe drops 60 tons of bombs on London

1940

Painting depicting the control-room at South West Regional Headquarters, Bristol, 1940, by John Piper. (IWM: ART LD 169)

Activities inside the receiver room of a Chain Home Low Station. (IWM: CH 15185)

7 SEPTEMBER London is subjected to bombing raids by more than 900 German aircraft; Göring views the air action from the Channel coast at Cap Gris-Nez, near Calais

8 SEPTEMBER Reuters reports the deaths of many civilians, mainly women and children, after a German bomb fell through the ventilation shaft of a London air-raid shelter

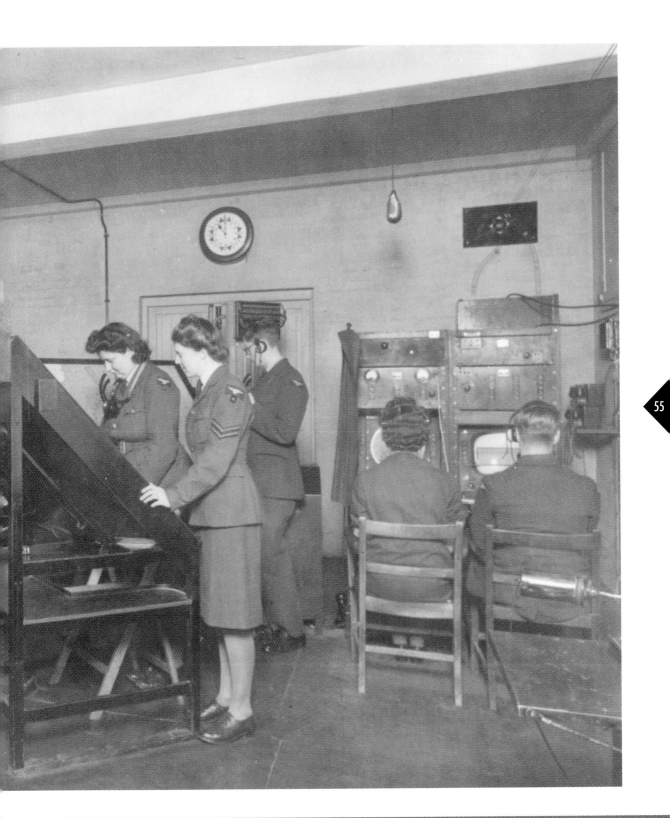

12 SEPTEMBER More than 1,000 German vessels berthed in French, Dutch and Belgian ports preparatory to a planned invasion of England are raided by the RAF; at least 80 barges are sunk in Ostend

14 SEPTEMBER The RAF causes further damage to German invasion matériel, with another series of raids, including a particularly successful one on Antwerp

that it must be something very secret. I don't think it was actually underground, but there were all these huts and things where we were taught. There was a table with the map of England on it and the whole of the map was marked out in a grid. The man on the other end of the telephone, when he was reporting things coming in, he'd give you, as far as I remember, two letters and four numbers and from that we put down a little round disc, like a tiddly-wink. Then a few minutes later there would be another one, that would be a bit further on and you could see the course gradually building up of something coming in.

You plotted everything. Everything came in over

WAAF fighter plotters are pictured hard at work in 'the Hole', Bentley Priory, the Headquarters of Fighter Command. (IWM: C 1870)

their radar tubes and the problem was to decide which was friendly and which was not. It was quite easy in the beginning because anything that was friendly went from England outwards and anything that was not came from France or Holland and Belgium inwards. We were on the other end of the radar stations, which were all round the east and southern coast of England – and which were responsible for controlling and winning, partly – as

15 SEPTEMBER On the day that the RAF scrambles all its fighters for the first time, the Germans lose 56 aircraft, almost 25 per cent of their force, compared to British loses of 26, signalling the failure of the Luftwaffe to gain control of the skies, which weakens the impetus for invasion; nowadays, this momentous date is celebrated in the UK as 'Battle of Britain Day'

*well as anything – the Battle of Britain. We had,
through this wonderful radar system forewarning of
any aeroplanes approaching our shores. We manned
the things twenty-four hours a day and night. We
used to be talking to these men who were sitting on
these outstations: 'Yes, they're coming now; there are
so many; now we can see them – think they're this
and think they're that – think there are so many.*

A WAAF radar operator plots aircraft on the cathode
ray tube. (IWM: CH 15332)

*Then, one day I was connected with the station
at Ventnor on the Isle of Wight where there was one
big station, and they saw these aircraft coming for
them. They actually switched off, they were being
attacked while I was actually talking to them. They
were badly – I think several people were killed – the
station was quite badly damaged.*

In 1940 thirty-seven-year-old **Jean Conan
Doyle** commanded the WAAF at Hawkinge
and West Kingsdowne.

We always had unit dances and things. And when

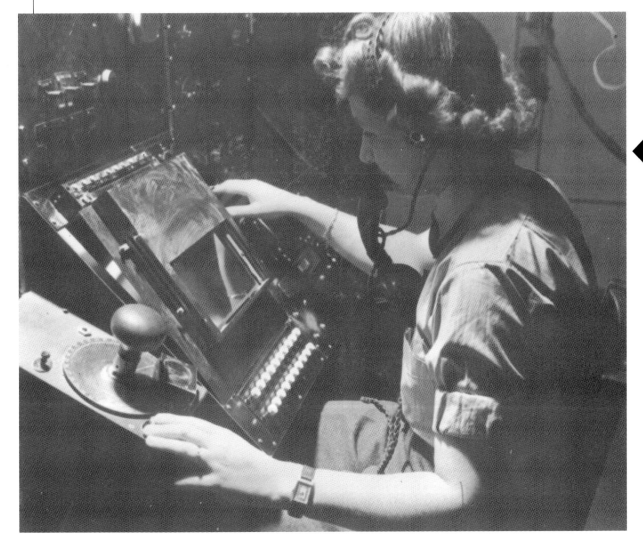

57

17 SEPTEMBER Hitler announces the
postponement of his proposed invasion of England

21 SEPTEMBER Though civilians have been using
London Underground stations as shelters since the
bombing raids began, the British government officially
grants permission for this practice to continue

1940

you went up to London you went to a lot of parties where you danced with Belgian officers, and Belgian officers all came up to you because we were all in uniform. Nobody waited for an introduction and one had a very social time. At West Kingsdowne there wasn't really any entertainment because the unit – the great majority were women, and very highly educated young women – found their entertainment off camp. They made friends with pilots at West Malling and other operational RAF units roundabout, or London. When they bombed that very, very famous restaurant the Embassy, we had some of our sergeants there at the time. Thank God they weren't killed.

In spring 1940 **Rosemary Horstmann** was a nineteen-year-old WAAF plotter at RAF Filton.

We sat round, or stood round, a large map table of the area, in the operations room. And with the aid of long sticks, like billiard cues, we pushed little symbols around on this table – showing enemy aircraft coming in, our aircraft going up to intercept them, and that sort of thing. We were hooked up by headphones to Observer Corps stations, and the Observer Corps people would telephone in to us with information about plots. There might be an unidentified something or other, and they would give us a grid reference, and we would put a little symbol on to that grid reference, and gradually the information would be built up.

In 1940, with the war intensifying, **Jean Mills**, now eighteen, was thinking about her part in the struggle. But one day she agreed

22 SEPTEMBER The RAF launches another bombing raid on Berlin

27 SEPTEMBER Germany, Italy and Japan sign a tripartite pact. Although Japan is still technically neutral, the agreement divides Europe and Asia into proposed 'spheres of influence' between the three countries

A scene of air combat from the Battle of Britain is captured on canvas by Paul Nash. (IWM: LD 1550)

The pin-up goes to war: sex very rapidly became part of the war effort, in magazines and newspaper cartoon strips.

30 SEPTEMBER The Luftwaffe delivers a final daylight raid on England, losing 47 aircraft to the RAF's 20. During September London was bombarded with over 6,000 tons of high explosive bombs and 8,500 tons of incendiaries

1 OCTOBER The fourth phase of the Battle of Britain is characterized by the Luftwaffe's series of night-time raids known as the 'Blitz', which puts a far greater strain on British ground defences and civil defences than daylight raids

1940

Occupants of the Operations Room of 10 Group, Box, Colerne. (IWM: CH 13680)

Air-Chief Marshal Sir Hugh Dowding, head of Fighter Command. It was mainly due to his strategic and tactical skill that Fighter Command was able to retain air superiority and ultimately thwart the Luftwaffe. (IWM: D 1417)

to accompany her mother on a shopping spree in London's West End. At Harrods, she encountered an armed forces recruiting drive, and ended up being sent to Leighton Buzzard as a WAAF trainee before being posted to RAF Duxford, where she found herself working in the operations room:

It was really dominated by a large table which was a

map. In the case of Fighter Command operations, it was the whole of the British Isles, but on individual fighter stations and groups it was more or less their area, with a slight overlap. This was a map with a grid like you would get on an Ordnance Survey of large squares and each large square was divided into 100 smaller ones, ten by ten, so it was possible to get a metric reading on that map. It was like a

7 OCTOBER Berlin is subjected to its heaviest raid by the RAF, when 30 Wellington and 12 Whitley bombers offload 50 tons of high-explosive bombs on the capital

11 OCTOBER The Luftwaffe bombs the port of Liverpool

graph and the plots came over to you as a metric reading like that, with a direction. It took quite a lot of getting into because when you hear unfamiliar voices coming in over the headset, coming in at quite a good speed, you have to concentrate fairly hard

until you're familiar with it. It came over like Northwest B for Bertie – that would be the name of the large square, the configuration of it and then it would be, say, one-nine-two-three, 1923, 20 at 10, which would be twenty aircraft at 10,000 feet.

From working as a plotter **Rosemary Horstmann** moved on to Hawkinge in Kent as a member of 'Y Service', which monitored the radio conversations between Luftwaffe pilots.

We had to be taught how to operate the receivers, how to search the band until we picked up some conversation or other, and how to tune in carefully. I still find myself doing this when I'm using the radio. Most people would just sort of switch it on, and just tune in like that. I still find myself searching backwards and forwards over the station, because I was taught to do it in 1940.

There was a 30,000-strong Observer Corps, the radar chain, and radio monitoring out of which came a web of information which could be fed to Anti-Aircraft Command and the pilots of Fighter Command, headed by Air-Chief Marshal Sir Hugh Dowding. And for a strategic view of German intentions there was the information coming in through Ultra to **Frederick Winterbotham** at Hut Three in Bletchley, centre of the Enigma decrypting operation.

One had to be able to get information quickly to Dowding, and I had a direct line from Hut Three put in to Fighter Command, and that was taken by a WAAF at the other end who had that sole job. They had two or three of them at the job of taking the Ultra signals and delivering them to the Commander-in-Chief. So Dowding was right on the ball. He knew exactly what was happening, because you would sometimes get advance notice of a big raid on a certain target with some hours to spare.

12 OCTOBER Hitler's planned invasion of England, Operation Sealion, is postponed until the spring of 1941

15 OCTOBER With the focus now on night bombing, Göring's main targets are aircraft manufacturing plants, the Midlands industrial region and London

1940

CHAPTER SEVEN

LAND AND SEA

EVEN BEFORE THE OUTBREAK OF WAR THE evacuation of city-dwellers, the vast majority children, to small towns and villages had begun. Around one and a half million people moved in the first autumn of the war. With the persisting phoney war many parents brought their children back, but the events of 1940 triggered another wave of departures. Rich and poor, town and country, northerners and southerners, West Country and East End were suddenly forced to face each other. The results were heartening, heartbreaking, farcical, tragic, disgraceful, shocking – and sowed the seeds of post-war social revolution.

Marshalled by a railway guard, a group of young Londoners enter a train bound for the West Country in June 1940. (IWM: TP 7089)

Ellen Harris witnessed the departures in north London.

The thing that stands out in my mind – quite early in the war, but it did bring tears to my eyes – were all the little children from the schools with their gas masks and the labels and the parents walking beside them, walking up to the station to be evacuated. That's the saddest thing that I think I could remember.

Lily Dytham was living in Wolverton, in Buckinghamshire and, working for the Women's Voluntary Service, could assess reaction to the prospect of housing evacuees.

It was mixed. Some were ready to take them, some didn't want to take them – I mean they didn't want the privacy of their homes taken away.

Clutching a gas mask and a bag of belongings, a small boy is in tears at the thought of leaving his London home.

These boys from Lowestoft were among thousands of children from East Coast towns and other areas under threat who were sent to reception areas in the west and Midlands. (IWM: HU 52715)

Surrounded by suitcases, a little girl is about to be evacuated from Chatham, Kent, in south-east England.
(IWM: HU 59253)

Two city boys from London enjoy a rural life in the Lake District.

22 OCTOBER In Belgium, squadrons of the Italian Reggio Aeronautica totalling 180 aircraft prepare for their first sorties against the British enemy

25 OCTOBER A British Air Ministry announcement reveals the deployment and training of airmen from Poland, France, Holland, Belgium and Czechoslovakia, showing the diversity of the Allied

Ernest Munson, a boy from West Ham in east London, found himself, not long before his ninth birthday, transported to Timberscombe in Somerset, and to the company of a whole new bunch of children.

There was always a little bit of needle, I suppose. But mostly we got on OK with them, being children I suppose they didn't hold too much malice for anybody else. Several things got blamed on the

Two young evacuees arrive at their new home in Amersham, Buckinghamshire.

pilots engaged in the air war; other countries represented are Canada, Australia, New Zealand, the West Indies, Ireland and the United States.

14 NOVEMBER Coventry is devastated during a 10-hour attack by the Luftwaffe, resulting in 500 deaths and 865 casualties, and the destruction of the city's medieval cathedral

1940

evacuee boys. I can remember one particular incident: a hayrick caught fire and that was blamed on the evacuee boys. I can remember a group of us boys walking from the village, the house where I was billeted was just on the outskirts of the village. It was about three-quarters of a mile up a small narrow road and we was walking up there just after we'd been delivered to Somerset, and one of the boys in his little Cockney accent said, 'Innit funny round here?' he said. 'There ain't no houses!' And there weren't. There was the house that we was billeted in, 200 yards down the lane was the mill, an old mill, just above that was a chapel, and then you got back into the village again, but from where we were stood you could only see one or two houses!

Distraught mothers at Waterloo Station, London, stand behind the barriers and watch their children leave for the relative safety of the country. (IWM: LN 4559C)

And that was strange. That was strange.

Lilias Woolven, aged twelve, was living in Hull and then evacuated to Scarborough.

I thought it was a great joke. You get into these school stories and you think, 'Oh it's just like a boarding school.' We were evacuated to a hotel, the Astoria, which overlooked the Italian Gardens

16 NOVEMBER In response to the attack on Coventry, the RAF launch assaults on a number of German and German-occupied cities, including Berlin, Bremen and Hamburg

17 NOVEMBER Air Marshal Sir Sholto Douglas replaces Dowding at RAF Fighter Command. The latter is reassigned to a minor position controlling aircraft supply, despite his skilful command of the RAF against the Luftwaffe. An uncomfortable

at Scarborough. They wouldn't do it now, but there were two girls to a bed and we were six in a bedroom. It was a very cold winter and everything froze up and there was no hot water in the place. One of my first memories is at the first meal that

A group of young Salford boys wait to be evacuated to the seaside resort of Blackpool, Lancashire.

character, Dowding's resistance to Churchill's pleas for more aircraft in the Battle of France probably ensured that for many years he never received the credit he deserved

20 NOVEMBER Birmingham and other Midlands towns and cities are subjected to night-time attacks by the Luftwaffe

we had at the hotel, which would have been the next day, we were all asked to hand over our sandwiches. For the dessert we got bread and butter pudding, but we didn't like the lettuce and the meat that was floating about in it. We spent Christmas at the hotel and we quite enjoyed it.

Lilias then went back to Hull, but with the city being bombed she was sent on to Bourne in Lincolnshire.

We were evacuated to houses there. Ours was that of a lady, Mrs Percival, who was quite delightful. She and her husband had no children of their own and they were very, very good. There we went to school in the morning and did nothing in the afternoon. It was a beautiful summer, we just went swimming and things like that.

She was then sent to Bingley, but, ill-treated and homesick, she returned to Hull.

There was an alternative. Through the Children's Overseas Reception Board evacuees were sent to North America, South Africa and Australasia. There were also privately organized departures. One of the latter was that of ten-year-old **Colin Ryder Richardson**, then living in Wales, who was to be sent to the United States and a wartime home in New York.

I think my father could see, with a huge German army standing on the French coast, there was what you might call a sense of urgency about going. Knowing the possibilities, the problems ahead, if the Germans did invade – and even I can hardly believe that they didn't actually do it, because the whole British army was in total disorganization after Dunkirk … why shouldn't they go straight through into Britain?

The chosen ship was the 11,000-ton flagship of the Ellerman Lines' *City of Benares*. On 13 September 1940 Colin Ryder Richardson was one of the ninety children amongst the 199 passengers and 209 crew who set sail from Liverpool as part of Convoy OB213 for Montreal. But by then, with the fall of France, the German U-boat fleet had moved into new bases in Brittany and were ranging far out into the Atlantic. But four days and 600 miles out into the ocean, the Royal Navy escort was withdrawn. Within hours *U48* had fired a torpedo at the British ship, not long after young Colin had gone to bed for the night.

68

1940

29 NOVEMBER Liverpool is severely bombed by the Germans

30 NOVEMBER Southampton endures an intense Luftwaffe air raid lasting seven hours

29 DECEMBER At least 10,000 fire-bombs are dropped by the Luftwaffe in a determined attempt to set fire to the City of London; large-scale fires blaze within parts of the City

There was a loud bang, a very loud bang, and almost immediately a smell of ... presumably cordite or something like that – it was an unmistakable smell. There were a lot of shouts so I immediately knew what was happening and I had a slight problem because I was in my pyjamas – my pink pyjamas – and I hadn't got my lifejacket, but I immediately put it on as I got out of bed, put on my slippers – and then I had a dressing gown and now I had a problem. Did I put the dressing gown under the lifejacket or on top of the lifejacket? It wouldn't go over the top of the lifejacket and things were beginning to happen rather fast. I thought I mustn't panic, on the other hand I must think these things through rationally.

Colin Ryder Richardson made his way to the assembly station. There was no panic on the stricken ship, despite a force 10 gale. The *City of Benares's* elderly nurse took him under her wing and they boarded a lifeboat – which promptly took water, immersing and numbing him up to his chest. Paradoxically, the waterlogging prevented that lifeboat suffering the fate of many of the others – capsizing. In appalling weather many of the ship's Lascar crew died immediately.

As the night wore on other survivors, clinging to the boat, or within the boat perished, from the freezing weather and choking in oil. Colin Ryder Richardson, clinging on to the old nurse, was befriended by John Day, a fifty-nine-year-old professor of economics at McGill University in Montreal:

He was gently suggesting to me that I should release the ship's nurse, as in his view she was dead, and I was so cold that really I couldn't really move my arms and legs. I was holding on for my life, holding on to her, and I really didn't want to let go of her because I felt that I would then lose whatever resource that I had in my arms, but it then became apparent to me that she was dying, and possibly was dead, and I still couldn't let go of her. I just felt that any minute we

might be rescued and there might be the possibility of life within her and it seemed to be so ... There was no need to let go of her – it would be cruel to let go of her. She was a person, even though she was patently dead and her mouth was open.

They said, 'Come on, Colin, let go of her, let go of her,' and I just couldn't do it. Eventually the storm solved the problem and she was swept away. We were getting fewer and fewer in numbers. There was a young man, a student, an Englishman as far as I know, who said he wanted something to eat or drink and he started drinking the seawater and everybody was telling him – the other people were telling him 'No', in between the waves, because it was very difficult to talk. The waves were just flowing over you. He was insistent on it and the next minute he jumped from the relative safety of the lifeboat into the sea.

After twenty hours Colin Ryder Richardson, described as a 'wisp of a Welsh boy' in the *Toronto Glove & Mail* was rescued, one of fourteen children out of the thirty-eight people in his lifeboat. Some 258 people from the ship died, including seventy-seven children. There was to be no more of the child evacuation programme. The inhabitants of the British Isles, men, women and children, remained, to await their fate.

One of the lifeboats containing the fortunate few to be rescued following the tragedy.

30 DECEMBER By the end of 1940, in spite of the heavy bombing endured by the United Kingdom, Hitler's strategy had failed to crush morale among civilians and the Forces; while the

RAF had completed mainly successful raids in Germany with few losses against less than effective defences

1940

CHAPTER EIGHT

BATTLE

THERE IS NO CONSENSUS ABOUT WHEN THE Battle of Britain started. And there was little coherence in Nazi deliberations about the when, whys, and hows of the projected invasion of Britain. But the German armed forces did have a way of destroying their opponents, and until summer 1940, that way had worked. It entailed air power, paratroopers and fast-moving armoured columns. But between the Wehrmacht and the shattered British Army lay the English Channel, and the Royal Navy.

Hermann Göring's Luftwaffe had to do to the RAF what had been done to the Dutch Air Force – outnumbered and flying obsolete planes – in a day: to destroy it. On 16 July 1940 Hitler ordered invasion plans to be drawn up within a month. In July the Luftwaffe tried, and failed, to draw Fighter Command into the Channel with attacks on shipping. On 6 August Göring drew up an action plan to destroy Fighter Command with a four-day campaign, and then bomb key targets, from the south coast to the Midlands. Two days later it ineffectively attacked radar stations. But, partly thanks to Ultra decryption, the British, amongst them **Frederick Winterbotham** in Hut Three at Bletchley had an idea of the overall German plan:

> *The vital Ultra signals of the Battle of Britain were the ones from Göring himself to his Luftflotten*

Adolf Hitler, leader of Nazi Germany, whose sweeping victories in Poland and in Western Europe left only one active opponent, Great Britain.

70

Dressed in blue, Reichsmarschall Hermann Göring was then Hitler's number two, and head of the German Air Force, the Luftwaffe.

commanders. Probably the most important signal we had, right at the beginning of the Battle of Britain, was Göring establishing his strategy with his commanders. He told them that they were to fly over Britain and bring the whole of the Royal Air Force up to battle, because only that way could it be destroyed in the time that they had. Now, that was the key for Dowding – to fight the battle with very small units every time they came over, and gradually wear them down, but always to have aeroplanes to

send up, because it became evident that Hitler and his generals wouldn't contemplate an invasion unless they had absolute control of the air over the Channel. We also got that intimated to us – and Göring's assurance to Hitler that this would be done – that he would bring Britain to its knees by his Luftwaffe alone. Now, this appeared in Ultra. And Churchill adored this because here was the whole strategy, and here was how we were going to fight the Battle of Britain, as we did.

Ultra helped with strategy. Radar focused tactics. Vitally, the Germans never understood its full significance, assuming that the RAF was fighting a decentralized

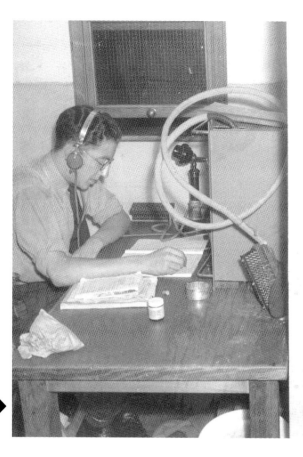

Radio operators take messages conveyed from the Intruder Squadron in action over enemy territory. (IWM: CH 7219)

battle. It was not, but on 12 August, and 13 August – Adlertag: the Day of the Eagles – the Luftwaffe launched a string of attacks on radar stations and RAF stations, like Manston, Lympne and Hawkinge, within the front-line area, within 11 Group. The Battle had irrefutably begun. Soon, while 11 Group concentrated on attacking the raiders, 10 Group to the west, and 12 Group to the north concentrated on protecting 11 Group's airfields.

Jean Mills, as a plotter at Duxford, was on the edge of 12 Group.

From the little rooms, the little wireless and radar rooms behind the controller, we could hear the crackling voices of the pilots come back and although we had headsets on and the work was quite

intensive and required a lot of concentration we used to manage to ease one earphone off so we could hear what was going on and then we could listen out for 'Tallyho', which meant they'd sighted the enemy, and then you could hear them talking to each other, like 'Look out, Blue Two, bandits to your right' and things like that, which seemed to bring it right into the room. There was an undescribable tension about the whole thing. When there was something going on the atmosphere was electric. We were all rooting for our boys to come back. They were very much our pigeon. It was a sort of combined effort as far as we were concerned.

11 MARCH The Lend-Lease Bill, under which Roosevelt's US government agrees to provide equipment, matériel and services to countries fighting the Nazis, is passed in Washington

13 MARCH Adolf Hitler announces his Directive for the invasion of Russia, although the decision and plans are maintained as a well-kept secret

But the Luftwaffe was not only attacking in the south. On 15 August **Hugh Dundas** was flying a Spitfire with 616 (South Yorkshire) Squadron, based at Leconfield, within 12 Group, on Humberside.

> We were sitting in the mess on that day, actually at thirty minutes' notice, when the tannoy went, and it told us in rather urgent tones to come to readiness. I'm not even sure it didn't tell us to scramble, which we thought was a very unorthodox message to receive while having lunch in the mess at thirty minutes' notice, but we put down our knives and forks and rushed out and got into cars and pushed off down to the field as quickly as we could.
>
> When we got there the operations clerk was jumping up and down and shouting for us to take off as fast as we could individually, just to get airborne. Off we all went in ones and twos. We were told on the R/T that there was a large force of German bombers approaching south of Flamborough Head – and there they were, a large force of German bombers, indeed of Dornier 17s, which were aiming for Driffield. We had quite a field day that day and succeeded in shooting down quite a number of those wretched aeroplanes, which of course hadn't got any escort and were in broad daylight, without any loss to ourselves.

A German Dornier DO-17 unloads bombs during the Battle of Britain.

16 APRIL London is subjected to a heavy all-night attack, as 500 German aircraft drop around 100,000 bombs on the capital, a total of 440 tons

8 MAY Hamburg and Bremen are subjected to a night-time attack by 359 RAF bombers

9 MAY In retaliation for the previous night's raid, Luftwaffe forces target the East Midlands' Rolls-Royce aircraft-engine factory, although contrary to reports broadcast on Radio Berlin the factory remains untouched and fully functional

1941

4

That same day **Roland Beamont**, was flying a Hurricane out of Exeter with 10 Group's 87 Squadron.

There were two squadrons at Exeter and one squadron at Warmwell, so our major battles were generally fought in that area with, at the most, three squadrons of Hurricanes and one squadron of Spitfires. You would not know that the other squadrons were there; you would be scrambled with nine, ten or twelve Hurricanes. A typical example was August 15, when my squadron was scrambled about four o'clock in the afternoon to intercept what was described by the controller as 'a hundred-plus heading north from Cherbourg'.

Pilots scramble to their Hurricane Mark I aircraft in response to an urgent call. (IWM: HU 2408)

We were vectored to Portland. We climbed out to Portland as quickly as we could and as we started heading south over Weymouth at about 15,000 feet, the controller was saying, 'Your hundred-plus is now 150-plus, twenty miles south of Portland Bill, heading north-east.' We thought, 'Right, they're just going to go up over Portland Bill and then turn left into a dive-bombing attack on Portland harbour,' which is exactly what they did.
We continued on our course. We had about

10 MAY In the final heavy mission of the Battle of Britain, London comes under attack from 550 Luftwaffe aircraft dropping high-explosive and incendiary bombs, which cause many fires and kill approximately 1,400 civilians; 27 German aircraft are lost. Since July 1940, however, the UK has endured more than 50,000 tons of German bombs and still stands firm, signalling to the Germans a significant turning point in their wartime fortunes

An artist's impression of Ju 87 Stuka dive-bombers in action during the Battle of Britain.

A squadron of German Stuka dive-bombers fly in formation.

nine aeroplanes that day. We were pulling our harness straps tight and turning on the gun sight and getting all the anticipatory moves necessary. Then the controller said, 'Bandits now twenty miles ahead of you, you should see them directly ahead.'

Almost immediately the clear sky ahead started to turn into a mass of little black dots. It could only really be described as a beehive – we used to call them the beehive. This mass of black dots appeared, developing, ahead. Our CO continued to lead us straight towards it. I just had time to think, 'I wonder what sort of tactic he's going to employ, is he going to turn up sun and try and dive out of the sun at them or go round to the right and come in behind ... what's he going to do?' While I thought that, it was quite apparent he wasn't going to do anything. He bored straight on into the middle of this

10 MAY Hitler's deputy and long-standing confidant, Rudolf Hess, secretly flies to Scotland, landing by parachute with peace proposals and guarantees declaring that Germany would respect the integrity of the British Empire if former German colonies were returned and Germany was granted a free hand in Europe

1941

lot until we seemed to be going into the biggest formation of aeroplanes you ever saw. Then his voice came on the radio and he said, 'Target ahead, come on chaps, let's surround them.' Just nine of us.

We went right into the middle. By that time we were no longer as inexperienced as we had been in France. I suppose many of us were now getting quite overconfident. We thought we were fully trained fighter pilots so there was less apprehension, there was more concentration and picking out a target. Out of this great mass ahead you would have two things to do. First thing would be to watch your immediate leader and make sure you didn't run into him, and you hadn't selected the same target as he had. In other words, if he was directly ahead of you it was no good trying to fire at his target because you might hit him. That wasn't regarded as a good thing to do.

You picked your own target, went in on a firing pass. Then with all this great mass of aeroplanes around, the next high priority was to avoid a collision because you would be diving into a mass formation.

They, in their turn, would start breaking formation under fire. The whole place would be a mass of aeroplanes going in all directions so you have to fire at a target and then try to evade anything that's in your way.

I fired at a Ju 87 at point-blank range and I hit it. I don't know what happened to it. I could see my tracers going into it, rolled away from it as I went by it, because I was going much faster than the Ju 87 Stuka. While I did that I came under attack from directly ahead and below. It turned out to be a Me 110 doing a zoom climb straight up at me firing as he came. He missed me. I rolled away from him straight behind another of his mates, a 110. I fired a long burst at him and his port engine stopped and started to stream smoke and fire and pulled away from that.

There seemed to be a lot of activity immediately behind my tail at that time so I went into a very tight turn, a diving turn, dived out of it until I seemed to be free of all the other aeroplanes, levelled out, climbed back up, and – as happened in that sort of

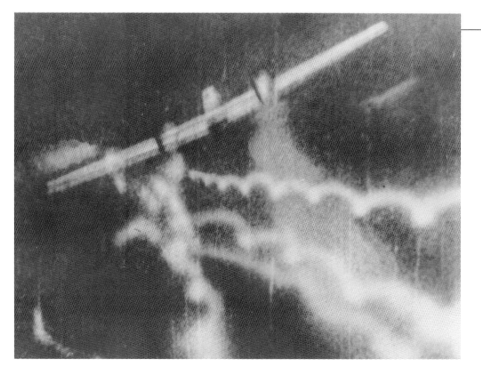

A camera-gun shot of fire from a British fighter striking a Messerschmitt 110. (IWM: C 1703)

11 MAY British air bases are the target for Luftwaffe raids, though many are revealed to be dummy installations

24 MAY The world's most powerful battlecruiser, HMS *Hood*, is sunk by Germany's 45,000-ton battleship *Bismarck*

Three Hurricane fighters flying in the classic British attack formation that was heavily criticized after the war.

confused fight – there was no sign of any Hurricanes. I could see a formation of aeroplanes in the distance which were probably the rest of the enemy heading off back across the Channel, and two or three streaks of smoke going down the sky where there were fires, burning aircraft. Then, immediately below – I was over Lyme Bay just south of Abbotsbury Swannery – I could see great boils in the water where either aircraft or bombs had gone in, I didn't know what they were. Then there was nothing else to do but go home because I was out

of touch with everything. I'd used most of my ammunition so I throttled back and opened the canopy, cooled down a bit, and flew off back home.

A key part of RAF tactics was the rotation of squadrons. So within a week of the action over Flamborough Head **Hugh Dundas** and his squadron had been transferred to Kenley in Surrey, where he was hit, possibly by British anti-aircraft fire.

The aeroplane ceased to function completely and went into a totally uncontrollable spin which it wouldn't come out of. I don't know really what the damage could have been but it would not recover from the spin. The engine was gone and there was

27 MAY The *Bismarck*, which Germany claimed was unsinkable, is sunk by the Royal Navy after a four-day pursuit

22 JUNE Operation Barbarossa begins without any formal declaration of war, as German forces enter the Soviet Union in a surprise invasion

1941

BOMBER COMMAND

19 JULY The BBC announces its 'V for Victory' campaign across Britain and occupied Europe to boost morale and give encouragement to the Allies

12 AUGUST Berlin endures its heaviest raid to date as RAF aircraft drop 82 tons of bombs on the city

Cover of a British government publication chronicling the activities of British bombers in action against targets in Western Europe.

Two Dornier 217s are pictured flying over the Woolwich Arsenal, London, in September 1940.
(IWM: C 5424)

a frightful lot of glycol smoke over everything. It took me a long time to get the hood open, we didn't have any quick-release toggles in those days. We had to pull it open, and somehow it had got a bit jammed. I couldn't get the bloody thing to open at all until I was a fairly long way down. I was at about 12,000 feet when we started. I finally got out of the beastly thing well under a thousand feet – because I was on to the ground, I would think, within twenty or thirty seconds of the aeroplane going into the ground. That was just north of Hawkinge.

The day that Dundas was shot down the first bombs fell on central London; a couple of days later, RAF Bomber Command hit Berlin, having earlier bombed Milan and Turin. Both sides produced inaccurate figures of each other's losses, but while the British assumed wrongly that there was plenty of Luftwaffe left, the Germans assumed, wrongly, the opposite about Fighter Command. This led Göring, at the beginning of September, to be told Fighter Command had 100 fighters left, when it had more than 700, and Fighter Command was being resupplied at a faster rate than the Luftwaffe.

Pilots like **Roland Beamont** could see what some of the Germans' problems were.

They were very limited in what they could do. Their bomber tactics were good – their dive-bombing with the Stuka 87 was very cost ineffective because their aeroplanes were very vulnerable. Spitfires and

14 AUGUST Churchill and US President Roosevelt hold a secret meeting and confirm a Western alliance with the signing of the Atlantic Charter

15 SEPTEMBER Rocket development at Peenemünde, on the Baltic coast, which had been previously suspended, is restarted by Hitler; work on the production of the V-2 rocket is given priority over naval and aviation requirements

1941

Hurricanes could shoot down Stukas like flies. They soon had to withdraw them because of their high loss rate. The way they used their Dorniers and particularly the Ju 88s as bombers was excellent. Their attacking accuracy was good. Their formation flying was very good. They produced quite powerful protective crossfire. Their fighter tactics – I think they were limited in two ways. One, they were at the extreme limit of their fighter operational range, they were operating from bases in northern France – they had to spend a lot of time forming up with the bombers. Then Göring's orders were that they were to stay rigidly with the bombers and not fly tactical manoeuvres round them. They were to fly in close proximity, in formation, with the bomber streams and only attack when attacked. That lost them a great deal of flexibility so they had very limited time over here, limited by fuel. And what time they had – they were limited by the tactics they were required to carry out. We learnt from that.

Among the neutral Americans reporting the conflict was Virginia Cowles from Boston, Massachusetts. A year after the Battle she wrote:

You knew the fate of civilization was being decided 15,000 feet above your head in a world of sun, wind and sky.

Such sentiments reflected the changed status of fighter pilots. On 20 August, with the Battle at its height, Winston Churchill famously told the House of Commons that 'Never in the field of human conflict was so much owed by so many to so few.'

Hugh Dundas noted the speech.

We all puffed our chests out a bit and thought how important we were, but until then, I don't think we thought about it particularly.

Pilots of No 19 Squadron, Duxford, are pictured leaping from a truck on the airfield following a call to scramble.
(IWM: CH 1398)

7 NOVEMBER Despite worsening weather and improved German air defences, Bomber Command continues to launch nightly air attacks, including a raid on Berlin by 169 RAF aircraft

30 NOVEMBER Hamburg is targeted by 84 RAF bombers, which drop 138 tons of bombs on the city; the first successful use of air-to-surface-vessel radar in action is made by a Whitley bomber which locates, bombs and sinks U206

Crowds view the wreckage of a German Heinkel
bomber, which crashed on the north-east coast of
Britain after an encounter with RAF fighters.

After Dunkirk, **Tony Bartley** was flying
with 92 Squadron and 11 Group. The public
were enthusiastic.

> They loved us. I mean loved. They bought you
> drinks, appreciated everything, they'd forgotten the
> acrimony that there was temporarily about the Army
> versus Fighter Command after Dunkirk. They
> realized, after what Churchill said – he sort of
> cooled it, and it was explained – and from then on
> in, I mean, the fighter pilot was – I don't know – you
> were absolutely the epitome of affection and
> clamour and idolatry – unbelievable. We knew that
> if Fighter Command was defeated, the operation, the
> landing which was being laid on, would go forward.
> Air superiority was the crux of the whole thing. If
> Great Britain lost air supremacy, if Fighter Command

was defeated the barges would come over to
England. The landings, the invasion forces would
come, the German armada would arrive.

Rosemary Horstmann, based with the
WAAF at Hawkinge in Kent, was at the
centre of the battle.

> There was a general feeling of elation. It was
> frightening, it was worrying – we used to see our
> own aircraft shot down, we would see German
> aircraft shot down, we would see parachutes opening
> over the countryside. But there was always this
> feeling, of . . . That we were jolly well going to win . . .
> I don't know that we knew very accurately what was
> happening. But there was a great sense of the
> gallant boys in blue arriving at dawn, you know. It
> was really rather like knights in armour on their
> trusty steeds. Their Spitfires and their Hurricanes.

Tony Bartley was flying out of Biggin Hill,
where on 30 August, in the most costly attack

7 DECEMBER Taking the land and seaborne
defences completely by surprise, the Japanese bomb
Pearl Harbor, Hawaii, which leads to the declaration
of war on Japan by the US

8 DECEMBER Britain and other Allied nations
also declare war on Japan

1941

on an air base during the Battle, thirty-nine personnel were killed and twenty-five injured.

> *We did five sorties a day, we never stopped, we just went. You went to your dispersal hut half an hour before dawn and you just – when the tannoy said scramble, you scrambled. You went up and you fought all day long until the sun went down. Whether it be three, four, five missions a day – you just fought and fought and fought. At the end of the day we got off the airfield, because they used to bomb us at night, so we would go down to the White Hart at Brasted and drink beer.*
>
> *And then the bombing got so bad after a while – the officers' mess was bombed – so we moved into temporary accommodation, which was an old army mess, it was a sort of prefab. And Fighter Command was so nervous, there would be three squadrons on the airfield but they said we couldn't live on the airfield at night so we were billeted in country mansions, three miles from the airfield, seventy-four went one way, we went another way, and there was another squadron there went another way. And we just lived off the airfield.*
>
> *So we just fought all day, and then we used to go to our billets just off the airfield because we were not allowed to – literally – to communicate with each other, because they were afraid that one bomb, if we were in the officers' mess together or the sergeants' mess together, the one bomb would knock off all the pilots of three squadrons. So we used to meet up when we were airborne. We never saw each other otherwise, we were segregated.*

In the month of August, 1,075 civilians had been killed, including 392 women and 136 children, and the casualty toll was getting worse.

In Southampton, on 13 August, bombers hit a cold store in the eastern docks. Eight-year-old **Eric Hill** had gone out with his mother.

> *We were in the bottom half of Southampton when the air-raid sirens blew and we had to dive for cover underneath the church, what they call the All Saints Church, and there was a terrific raid going on above. I remember we were in the air-raid shelter for three, four hours until we got the all-clear to come out. There was a cosmopolitan lot of people, shoppers mostly, in there and I always remember vividly when we came out the high street was running with melted margarine and butter because they'd hit the cold storage. And I remember my mother and most of the women – because it was wartime – they were just grabbing handfuls of this butter and try to ram it into whatever they could so we could have butter or margarine.*

Firemen tend to a blaze in a collapsed building after a bombing raid on Southampton.

11 DECEMBER Hitler declares war on the United States; in response the US announces its own declarations of war against Germany and Italy

31 DECEMBER Despite suffering catastrophic losses, and losing vast tracts of territory to the invaders, the Soviet Union manages to hold its position on the Eastern Front at the end of 1941, having driven the Germans back in some places and narrowly prevented them from taking Moscow

The International Cold Store was to burn for two weeks, and the town reeked of margarine. On 4 September Hitler ordered the Luftwaffe to focus on cities as war targets and three days later, on Saturday afternoon, in a daylight raid three waves of bombers hit London, killing 448 civilians and injuring 1,600. The raids continued all night: the Battle of Britain was not over, and the night-time Blitz had begun.

The following seven days, culminating in the big raids of Sunday, 15 September, were to prove, in retrospect, decisive. In command of 11 Group, which encompassed south-east England, where the main battles were taking place, was the New Zealander Air Vice-Marshal Keith Park. **Frederick Winterbotham:**

I think the final day raids on London, when Göring was going to have his final whack at London – he ordered practically the whole of the bombers that were left in France to come over and bomb London – was a coup de grâce, because if he couldn't down the Air Force, he'd down the population. And we got good advance information about that.

Churchill was told about it, and he went down to the headquarters of 11 Group. He didn't go to Fighter Command where Dowding was. He went down to number 11 Group, to Keith Park's, to watch this battle. And Dowding had collected every fighter aeroplane left in Britain. In fact he'd brought them down to the Midlands, he'd brought them up from the west of England and he'd assembled every Spitfire that we'd got left. And when this vast formation came over in the daytime – we had the time they were coming – he sent up every Spitfire that he'd got. And this time he hadn't got to bother about keeping the Air Force so much intact. But they completely shocked the vast German air fleet that was coming over, and they just turned round and fled and dropped their bombs.

The Ultra which came from Göring really almost

Illustrated in an Italian newspaper, Heinkel III bombers engage in daylight raids on London's docks, but are prevented from conducting low-altitude attacks due to the presence of protective barrage balloons.

burnt the paper. They were to turn round, refuel their aeroplanes and go back and bomb London. Churchill had been down with Keith Park and, seeing the enormous formations that were coming over on the radar and the plotting, he turned to Keith Park and said, 'What reserves have you got?'

Keith Park said, 'Perhaps you'd better ask the Commander-in-Chief, sir.'

So the Commander-in-Chief was telephoned at Stanmore and asked, 'What reserves have you got?' And Dowding's remark, 'I have no reserves, sir, every aeroplane is in the sky'... that put old Churchill in his place. They came back on that evening; they didn't even get as far as London. They just turned

22 FEBRUARY Air Marshal Sir Arthur Harris is appointed chief of RAF Bomber Command. The force moves towards the mass area bombing of German cities. Civilian casualties will be huge.

26 MARCH 200 RAF bombers are launched in a heavy raid against the important industrial towns of the Ruhr Valley in Germany

1942

round and fled again, and that was the end of daylight raiding in England. They were great days, but my goodness, it was hard work.

The British claimed to have downed 185 German aircraft. **Elizabeth Quayle:**

I remember there was enormous elation on the 15th of September. I now know that there were far less aircraft shot down than we thought, the numbers we fed were double or very nearly double. There were moments of great elation.

On that day the British had shot down 60 aircraft – 26 fighters and 34 bombers – and severely damaged another 20. From 7 September to 15 September the Luftwaffe lost 199 bombers and 99 fighters, the RAF 120 fighters. Daylight bombing was becoming

Firemen put out flames on a London street following an air raid on 11 September 1940. (IWM: FX 10941)

During a bomb attack in September 1940, an empty bus is blasted against the front of a house in Mornington Crescent, Camden Town. (IWM: HU 3194)

1942

29 MARCH Now in service with Bomber Command, the new Lancaster bomber is deployed in a devastating raid on the ancient city of Lübeck

24 APRIL In retaliation for the bombing of Lübeck, Hitler orders an attack on Exeter

25 APRIL Bath is the target of another reprisal raid; York, Hull and Norwich come under attack in subsequent raids

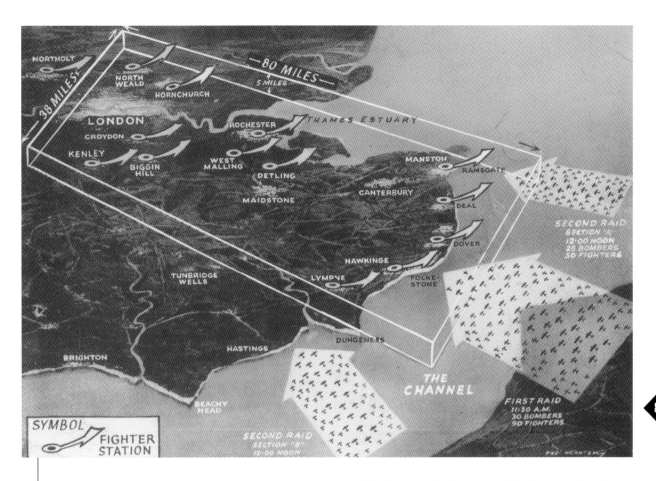

A bird's-eye view of the Battle of Britain shows the area of conflict across south-east England. The two great raids here illustrated arrived on the morning of September 15 1940; two more followed in the afternoon. (IWM: HU 1857)

an unaffordable luxury for the Germans. The air superiority needed to launch an invasion had not been won. Sealion was postponed, and postponed. The British Isles were not to be invaded. Democracy survived in Europe. The tactics of the New Zealander Keith Park at 11 Group had been vindicated, and so had the strategy of Sir Hugh 'Stuffy' Dowding.

Elizabeth Quayle:

I think we all admired Stuffy, our Stuffy, enormously.

We had great loyalty to him. I think you might call it affection, he built up a tremendous – well, it's an old-fashioned word – esprit de corps amongst us. He was a gentleman, quite frankly.

Tony Bartley:

September 15 I was flying. I did five sorties on that day, the crunch when Göring just gave up. They said, 'We can't beat them.' And so they gave up the huge onslaught because their losses were so terrific. I may say ours were too. Then they called off the invasion – they decided, and then of course the weather came down, thank God. Day after day in September we were rather longing, towards the end, for the beginning of October, for the cloud, because we were getting desperately tired, we never stopped. We never, never, stopped.

30 MAY 'Bomber' Harris orders a major raid on Cologne involving more than 1,000 bombers, using almost every serviceable RAF bomber aircraft, and offloading more than 2,000 tons of bombs; with a total of only 40 aircraft lost, RAF chiefs claim to have destroyed more than 200 factories

1942

CHAPTER NINE

SEALION DROWNED

IT WAS IN THE MONTHS, AND YEARS, AFTER THE September 1940 defeat of the Luftwaffe that the measure of what had been achieved in what became known as the Battle of Britain was realized. But in the autumn of 1940, for the people of the British Isles, the threat of invasion remained and persisted into 1941. For people like **Frederick Winterbotham**, however, with access, through Ultra, into

Hitler's thinking, the situation was different. *As a result of all our pre-war knowledge of Hitler's intentions, and through Ultra, we were getting some of his preparations for the Russian invasion. We were aware that if he was going to invade Russia early in 1941, he would have to either invade or leave it alone by September, as regards England. So we got a date very neatly by mid-September – we knew that if they didn't invade by then, they wouldn't*

Published in the French edition of the German magazine *Signal* in 1941, a map reveals targets for the Luftwaffe. The brown areas are mining districts, the red stars are ports and the circles indicate factories.

Des buts sur l'île d'Angle-terre

Cette carte d'Angleterre montre les buts qui ont été exposés, jours et nuits, aux puits des bombes allemandes, et qui le seront encore : des ports militaires, des chantiers, des garnisons, des stocks d'huile et des silos de blé, des usines d'armement, des mines de charbon et de fer, des usines d'acier et d'aluminium. Pendant que la marine de guerre allemande coupe toute communication et que l'encerclement de l'île se fait de plus en plus efficace, l'arme aérienne atteint les autres centres vitaux de l'adversaire à l'intérieur de l'île, qui sont d'une première importance pour la guerre et qui sont répandus sur le pays entier

A painting depicts the stealthy advance of German panzers with air support from Stuka dive-bombers.

come at all. We got this signal from Hitler giving permission to dismantle the air loading bays in Holland. Now, that seemed a fairly harmless sort of operation, but as we knew exactly how the operation was going to take place, and they wouldn't invade unless they had all this proper air support, it was tantamount to saying the invasion was off. That signal I sent straight through to Churchill, and it went to the Chiefs of Staff.

Churchill ordered a conference down in the underground room beneath the Foreign

Office. Amongst those present were Major-General Hastings Ismay, Churchill's link with the Chiefs of Staff, Air-Chief Marshal Sir Cyril Newall and Sir Stewart Menzies, head of the Secret Intelligence Services and superior of **Frederick Winterbotham**.

Major-General Hastings Ismay (right), Churchill's Chief of Staff, his personal representative to the Chiefs of Staff's Committee and his closest military adviser during the Second World War. General Sir Alan Brooke is seated at left, next to Air-Chief Marshal Sir Charles Portal. (IWM: BU 9104)

I was commanded to go along with my boss as the producers of this signal, and explain it to them. It was one of the most extraordinary moments of my life, and of the war, I think, because there down below were all the Chiefs of Staff and a few secretaries and the Prime Minister and General Ismay and my chief and myself.

And this signal was in front of Churchill, and he said, 'Well, gentlemen, we'd like to know what this really means.' And Menzies was called upon – he told me because I'd studied the whole thing, he didn't know what was going on really. And I pointed out that if these loading bays were dismantled it meant that they

would not have their proper air support and that in fact Hitler had given up the idea of invasion.

So Churchill looked at me, and then he turned to Chief of Air Staff: 'May I have your views?' he said to Cyril Newall, and Newall said, 'That is entirely our view, with the dismantling of this, the invasion is off.'

Everybody sat back in their chairs, like that, because the Chiefs of Staff, the Army and the Navy, they didn't really know what this was about. And Churchill sat back and smiled, and pulled out a big cigar and lit it.

1 JUNE The raid on Cologne is followed by a 1,036-strong bombing attack on Essen

3 JUNE US ships and carrier-borne aircraft engage Japanese naval forces in the Battle of Midway, resulting in the withdrawal of the Japanese fleet, with heavy losses, four days later

Prime Minister Winston Churchill, in the pose that projected the image of a defiant country worldwide.

Air-Chief Marshal Sir Cyril Newall, Chief of the Air Staff from 1937-40, whose ideas for developing the RAF included the Home Air Force and Bomber Command units, in order to maintain parity with Germany.

21 JUNE Tobruk in Libya falls to Rommel's Afrika Korps, with the loss of more than 20,000 Allied prisoners

26 JUNE Bremen is hit in an RAF bomber raid of more than 1,000 aircraft

1942

CHAPTER TEN

BLITZ

IN THE AUTUMN OF 1940 **JEAN MILLS** WAS working in the operations room at RAF Duxford, near Cambridge.

We were on duty one night and it had been fairly quiet. That's the thing – there were periods of absolute inactivity when you had to do something to keep yourself from being bored. Suddenly we looked, and one girl stood up and put a plot way out in the North Sea. In no time at all there was a whole row of plots coming, and then the sergeant of the watch conferred with the commanding officer and they removed all the individual plots and put a long stretch of cardboard, covering several hundred miles.

It was a 300-plus-mile front of bombers coming. We began to wonder what was going to happen and in which way they were going to go.

The Battle of Britain was conflict in light. The Blitz was darkness, illuminated by fire. Daytime bombing meant unacceptable losses for the Luftwaffe. Its response was an escalation of the night-time raids which had begun in summer 1940 and went on to produce a winter of horror, death, demoralization – and heroism. The losses of the Luftwaffe were negligible. And the

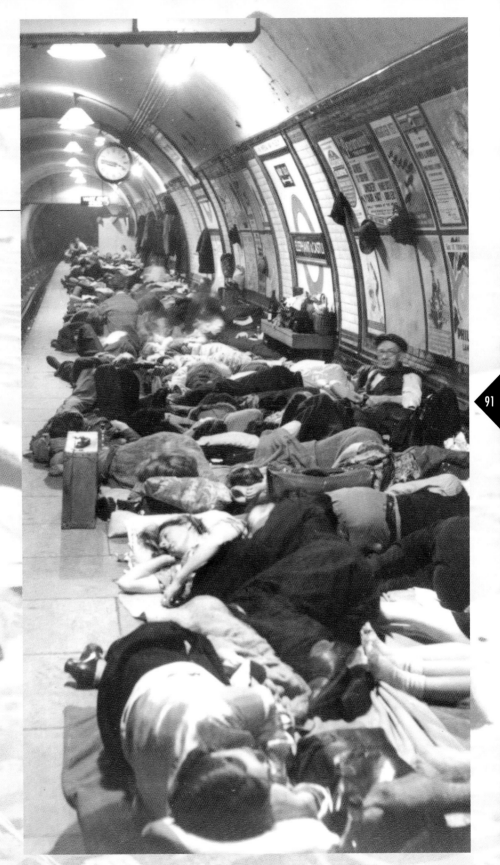

People sleep on a platform at Elephant and Castle underground station, in November 1940.
(IWM: D 1568)

The dramatic night-time attack on a Bristol Beaufort by a German fighter, captured in a painting published in *Signal*.

A Heinkel III bomber, the same type of German aircraft shot down by navigator William Gregory in August 1940.

Germans had the 'Beam'. Thanks to continental radio beacons German pilots could check their positions – and they were flying along a radio beam which kept them on course. **Frederick Winterbotham:**

> *The Beam consisted of one beam sending out dots all the time, and another beam some miles away, at a different angle sending out dashes. So you flew your aeroplane along and you heard dots on one side and dashes on the other. But when they came together and you heard one note, you knew you were over the target.*

The British met with some success in 'bending' the Beam. But it was not enough and at night Spitfires and Hurricanes were almost useless. The Observer Corps could see little, inland radar was minimal and initially the RAF's night-fighter squadrons largely relied on an inadequate converted bomber, the Bristol Blenheim. On 18 August 1940 twenty-seven-year-old **William Gregory** was the navigator with Pilot Officer Rhodes, flying a Blenheim out of Digby and Wellingore in Lincolnshire.

4 JULY USAAF units based in Britain take part in their first action during a combined attack with the RAF on Dutch airfields used by the Luftwaffe

6 JULY General Auchinleck, Commander-in-Chief Middle East, takes personal command of Eighth Army and first halts, then drives back Rommel's forces in the First Battle of El Alamein. Auchinleck's

A Luftwaffe bomb leaves a large crater in the centre of the street between the Royal Exchange and the Bank of England in London.

There was no radar, it wasn't until the introduction of airborne radar and ground control radar that the nightfighter came into its own world. We were scrambled at night and the ground, the sector, used to come to you over the air and say, we have a plot that is near you. Well this night they told us there was a plot given by the Observer Corps very near to where we were. I was in the gun turret looking round and I didn't see anything. We came out of a cloud at about 10,000 feet, I would think, and immediately behind us

came this German aircraft, with its cockpit light on, a Heinkel 111. I didn't know who was the most scared, the pilot or the gunner in the Heinkel, or me, but I pressed the trigger, first 100 rounds into the cockpit, and it started to flame and it came underneath and Rhodes finished it off and shot it down.

Such success was a rarity as Britain went on to face the Blitz. One night at RAF Duxford, sixty miles away from London, **Jean Mills** arrived on duty at 4 a.m.

As we approached through the guardroom we saw this great glow in the sky to the south-east. It was absolutely red, like the biggest sunset you ever saw, a long way away, and we said to the guard, the sentry,

'What on earth's that? What's going on?'

He said: 'Oh, that's London burning.'

I think that was the first big incendiary raid on the docks – when they got the margarine factories. And for the first time you really felt it in the pit of your stomach, and thought, 'Oh my goodness.'

Elizabeth Quayle was based at RAF Fighter Command headquarters at Bentley Priory in Stanmore, Middlesex until November 1940, but also worked with Air Raid Precautions (ARP).

It is very difficult to explain what London was like. First of all, everything was blacked out. You couldn't

see. When you were actually trying to find your way – where you'd been sent with your ambulance, you know, someone would say 'Hoy! There's a great crater there. Don't go there, go somewhere else.' It was quite an experience. All down the East End it was absolutely chronic. We dreaded, or at least I did, when the moon was up – you always hoped there would be a cloud cover and that they wouldn't be able to follow the Thames: they could see this great silver ribbon below them and they used it to follow it, and come up, and drop their bombs.

The raids built up as the winter progressed. At the end of December 1940, 136 bombers attacked the City of London with high explosives, parachute mines and incendiaries. **Frederick Winterbotham** was heading out of the metropolis.

And as I went out in my car, westwards towards my cottage in Berkshire, I could turn back to see the whole of the City in flames around St Paul's Cathedral, which was a terrible sight. And I was just looking out of the back window when my driver swerved violently up a side street. Just in time, because a bomb exploded just in front of us. That was the sort of night one put up with in London.

That night too a reporter on a national daily, the *News Chronicle*, thirty-five-year-old **Stanley Baron** went to investigate. It was just after the all-clear had sounded.

I decided to walk round London. It was on fire. All the buildings round St Paul's were on fire. The Guildhall was on fire. Whenever one looked up the narrow alleys of the city you saw what it really looked like. I think I described it at the time as red

---

Following a night-time bombing raid by the Luftwaffe, firefighters are depicted working in vast numbers to extinguish flames engulfing the industrial areas of London.

19 AUGUST Almost 6,000 Allied troops, mostly Canadians, are involved in a disastrous attempt to raid Dieppe; the landing is completed, but only a fraction of the targeted installations are attacked for the loss of many lives and some 1,500 prisoners, as well as aircraft, tanks and landing-craft

The spirit triumphant: St Paul's Cathedral survives the London Blitz while surrounded by the flames from burning buildings nearby which redden the sky.

snow storms. Great showers of sparks were coming from the burning buildings. And you would see the silhouette sometimes of a fireman.

And I remember particularly the silhouette of the fireman at the Guildhall. I managed to get just inside the entrance of the Hall while it was still on fire. Firemen told me that Gog and Magog were burning. And looking up from outside the building I saw the quite extraordinary picture of the silhouette of a fireman on a high water-tower and his jet illumined by the flames from the building.

25 AUGUST The Duke of Kent, youngest brother of King George VI and a serving RAF officer, is killed in an aircraft crash

8 SEPTEMBER German Sixth Army confronts an entire Soviet army in Stalingrad, so beginning the siege

1942

What struck me most about that night was the extraordinary beauty of it. It sounds fantastic. But it really was a very beautiful scene. The colours were fantastic. St Paul's itself – the dome of St Paul's – was to be seen against a background of yellow and green and red with great billows of smoke coming across it. And at the Guildhall the silhouette of this fireman was similarly black against this extraordinary glowing sky. Before the war I had walked around most of the City. I loved the City, and I knew its buildings. And there I was, simply watching the whole thing burn. And that is the thing which I have remembered very clearly all my life.

In November 1940 a new word flared into the European vocabulary, 'coventrate'. It defined what had happened when more than 400 Luftwaffe bombers destroyed the Midlands

25 SEPTEMBER RAF Mosquitos conduct a low-level bombing raid on Oslo, targeting the Gestapo office with great success, and destroying the HQ along with its records of Norwegian resistance fighters

24 OCTOBER The Battle of El Alamein begins when General Montgomery orders a 1,000-gun bombardment of the German positions and minefields, followed by a night-time attack

The ruins of Coventry Cathedral which was destroyed in a shattering raid on the city in November 1940. Only the spire remained standing.
(IWM: SG 14860)

The city of Coventry is devastated during a relentless night-time bombing raid by the Luftwaffe.
(IWM: H 5597)

city – between eight in the evening and dawn – and dangled the prospect of what lay ahead for the world, east and west, Allied and Axis. It was London, it was Coventry that winter, but it was also Birmingham and Bristol and Sheffield and Portsmouth and Plymouth and Manchester and Belfast and Glasgow and Cardiff and Swansea and even neutral Dublin by accident.

And for eight-year-old **Eric Hill** the real Blitz came to Southampton that November.

4 NOVEMBER Following Montgomery's successful breakthrough of the Afrika Korps' front line at El Alamein on 3 November, Rommel is reported to be in full retreat

29 NOVEMBER Speaking from London in a radio broadcast, Churchill addresses all Italians involved in the war, telling them they have to choose between the overthrow of Mussolini or a major Allied attack

Through German eyes: a Sheffield factory crumbles under Luftwaffe attack.

A Bristol Beaufighter launches a rocket attack in enemy territory.

A group of young children from Southampton whose homes were damaged in the bombing raids await evacuation to safer areas in December 1940. (IWM: HU 49423)

17 JANUARY London is subjected to a night-time raid by German bombers, totalling 118 aircraft, for the first time since May 1941

30 JANUARY While the German Air Ministry in Berlin commemorates the tenth anniversary of Hitler's regime, British Mosquito fighter-bombers

That's when Southampton was devastated. We lived about four miles from the centre in a place called Bassett. Naturally they all put us in the air-raid shelter. The Messerschmitts, and the Dornier bombers seemed to come right over the estate that I lived on, and turn round, and dive-bomb Southampton. All we could see was the town ablaze – you could just see

the glow – we knew that Southampton was really getting hammered.

And then there was an incident just before my father got called up. There was no air-raid siren blown that night, but you could tell the different sounds of the aeroplanes' engines. You knew the Dornier had a sort of gnawing, groaning sort of effect. My father rushed in

launch a daylight raid on the German capital, hitting the radio broadcasting building with two aerial mines

5 MARCH The Krupp munitions factory at Essen is raided by aircraft from RAF Bomber Command comprising Lancaster, Halifax, Stirling and Wellington bombers; marking the start of regular action against Germany's industrial centre, the Ruhr Valley

1943

and threw my mother and me underneath the kitchen table and we heard an almighty explosion. It was a landmine on a parachute, it landed in the next road and killed several families there and I remember my father, and all the neighbours, went up to assist all they could. I was too young, obviously, to go. That was in Bluebell Road. I lived in a road called Lilac Road, and this was Bluebell Road.

You can always tell, to this day, where the bomb – the landmine – landed, because you have got a road full of 1930s-style houses and then you have got, in between, about three houses that are more or less modcon where they rebuilt it.

In the blitzed city of Liverpool, a fire engine crashes into a crater, injuring several firemen. (IWM: PL 227A)

By March 1941 RAF nightfighter squadrons, although still few in number, were re-equipping with the rugged and efficient Bristol Beaufighter. **William Gregory** was navigator and radar operator with pilot Ken Davidson on one of the new planes, and still flying out of Digby and Wellingore in Lincolnshire.

We were on patrol one night when the ground came

19 APRIL British Intelligence is informed of an increase in the research and testing of rockets in Germany, which leads to a request for photo-reconnaissance of the Peenemünde site

12 MAY All organized Axis resistance in North Africa ends with the surrender of German and Italian forces there

Anti-aircraft guns in action in Hyde Park, London.

through to say Liverpool was getting blitzed. When we arrived in the Liverpool area you could see the glow of the fires through the clouds, and we were at about 10–15,000 feet. We called up different people and no one replied, and I switched on the radar – and found a contact so we closed in. It was a Dornier 17, and just as this chap Davidson was about to shoot it down, our starboard wing was shot off by ack-ack. I bailed out and landed on a

little place next to Lime Street Liverpool, and he landed inland some place.

I was on the roof of this house for about ten minutes when a ladder came up to the eaves and a chap came up the ladder with a gun.

I said, 'Thank God you can get me off.' And I was fastened on to a chimney pot I had held on to.

And he said: 'You bloody German, you can speak as good English as we.' And he said: 'When you get on the ground you'll find that out.'

So they started to put the boot in when I eventually got down. They had every right, when you saw the fires that were going on. I was in full Irving

17 MAY RAF Lancaster bombers carry out the 'Dambusters' raid, bombing and partly destroying two major dams, the Möhne and Eder, causing considerable damage within Germany's industrial heartland

23 MAY More than 2,000 tons of bombs are dropped over Dortmund by 754 RAF aircraft; Air-Chief Marshal Harris reveals that a total of 100,000 bombs have been dropped on Germany to date

1943

Printed in the Italian magazine *Illustrazione del Popolo* in October 1940, London's Docklands comes under heavy fire from the Luftwaffe.

One night – I don't know what had happened – we must have gone round the country and gathered up every gun plus the ones that were being made and we let fire on the enemy. And I've never known anything so morale-boosting. Everywhere the next day 'Wasn't that wonderful? They've got the guns, they're going to keep them out.' It did have its effect.

On 5 December 1940 the Nazi propaganda minister, forty-three-year-old Joseph Goebbels, wrote in his diary that Southampton was 'one single ruin', continuing: 'So it must go on until England is on her knees, begging for peace.' Little **Eric Hill** was an inhabitant of the ruin.

There was hardly anything standing at all in the bottom part of Southampton. They didn't do a lot of damage to the docks – there was virtually very little damage to the docks. It was more or less the residential areas and the shopping areas that got the main bit of the German Luftwaffe – as they call it now – carpet bombing. They just blitzed anything. They came over – I don't think there was any specific

kit in those days – Irving jacket and Irving trousers and when they ripped the coat off I was in RAF blue underneath.

I was a 'bloody spy'!

Eventually a police chap came up and took me to the police station and I put a call through to my squadron at Digby and they sent a car out, found Ken Davidson and we came back together.

Other than shooting down RAF planes, the anti-aircraft guns could be morale boosters, as **Ellen Harris** found in London:

1943

23 JUNE An aerial reconnaissance mission over the Peenemünde site yields photographic evidence of rocket production

28 JUNE Cologne is badly damaged during a bombing raid involving more than 500 British aircraft; despite a six-month period of heavy bombing by the RAF, production of munitions and aircraft is still being maintained at a high level in Germany

10

Strength and light: Dame Laura Knight's classic depiction of a barrage balloon site in Coventry, 1942, indicates how women's lives have changed for ever.
(IWM: LD 2750)

People gather at the end of a London street to view the pile of rubble that used to be their homes.

target, they used to come, 'We're over Southampton, bomb doors open,' and away went the bombs.

Across Britain a defence of sorts against the bombers was provided by the Anderson Shelter, named after the Home Secretary Sir John Anderson who had put together the scheme for the two-bunk corrugated steel garden shelters. Thirteen-year-old **Lilias Woolven** was back in Hull after her unhappy evacuation to Bingley.

There was some pretty nasty bombings started and we used to have to sleep in this Anderson shelter. We'd got bunk beds and were supposed to take proper shelter bedding out there, and we had special sheets – I don't think we had such things as sleeping bags in those days. I suppose we had

10 JULY British and US forces invade Sicily in the largest seaborne invasion of the war

12 JULY The German army is routed in the Battle of Kursk, the greatest tank battle ever fought

eiderdowns and blankets. One night the sirens sounded and we went out into the shelter and I was suddenly aware amongst other things – the noise, the guns and the bombs – of this swishing noise. It was a landmine that was drifting over the house, and it exploded in Scarborough Street, just off Hessle Road, and it was pretty close – it brought the windows in and the ceilings down, and the door, but we weren't bombed out of anything; they soon came and patched up the windows.

In north London the family of **Ellen Harris** had their own early warning system for

The Nazi propaganda minister, Joseph Goebbels, is pictured speaking at a rally in 1940.

A grocer's shop is wrecked by a bomb, but the Anderson shelter that took the full force of the bomb stands intact. (IWM: HU 48554)

1943

15 AUGUST Having completed the conquest of Sicily, Allied forces invade the mainland of Italy

17 AUGUST The German rocket research site at Peenemünde is attacked by the RAF, suffering enough damage to delay progress there for a few weeks

departure to the shelter.

> *We had a cat who used to tell us before it arrived that an enemy plane was on its way, before we heard it. The cat would scurry from the side entrance, up the garden, and down into the shelter. And we'd hear in a very short time. We'd be scuttling across the ground to follow the cat. Always this happened.*

Eric Hill:

> *It was no good going to bed because as soon as you got in the bed, air-raid sirens used to go. So what we all decided – the people in the road – we all made the shelters as comfortable as we could and we used to virtually sleep in the air-raid shelter all night because at least you were already there and you were safe . . . well, comparatively safe.*

In London, safer still as a shelter, if excessively communal for some, was London's tube system. The government attempted to block its use by the public, but soon abandoned that folly. **Elizabeth Quayle** took the train.

> *When you came back at night on the underground, of the entire platform, only the bit – the eighteen inches or maybe two foot near the rail – was left, and all the rest were rows of people with their belongings, cats and dogs and children. They were as good-tempered as it was possible to be. Looking back on it, everyone was much more friendly – you would have thought nothing of leaving your bags or your suitcase there; nobody would have taken anything.*

Black people had lived in London for generations. With the war, people like the Jamaican-born doctor Harold Moody found themselves tending fellow victims of the Blitz. Many more blacks arrived with the armed forces of the West Indies and Africa. They encountered racism, gratitude, abuse, friendship and simple ignorance. As **Ellen Harris** realized:

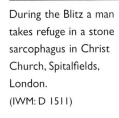

During the Blitz a man takes refuge in a stone sarcophagus in Christ Church, Spitalfields, London.
(IWM: D 1511)

8 SEPTEMBER Italy's unconditional surrender and armistice with the Allies is announced. Mussolini is imprisoned on the order of the provisional government, but is dramatically rescued by German commandos four days later

22 SEPTEMBER Hanover is the focus of a raid by over 650 RAF bombers dropping more than 2,300 tons of bombs on the city

1943

We are a multi-racial country, so much is now accepted. But going back to the time of the raids, I wakened one morning in my shelter to find a great, big black man sleeping next to me. I was horrified, to say the least – true. But my father was with me on the other side so all was well. But the question of colour or type of person, class – entirely – it all went by the board. We were all fighting a war and we were all helping each other in whichever way we could. Everybody felt they were all in this. My husband was ARP, my sister-in-law was a firefighter

London citizens sleeping in an underground station to keep safe from nightly bombing raids, in a scene similar to that described by Elizabeth Quayle.

Londoners are depicted removing valuables and important documents from offices, and sandbagging buildings to protect them against further bomb attacks.

27 SEPTEMBER Hanover is targeted in another huge attack by RAF bombers. The focus of the raid is the Continental tyre works, but this factory and other war-related industrial sites are barely hit in the attack

22 OCTOBER The Fiesler aircraft factory at Kassel is raided by 486 RAF bombers, following the discovery by British intelligence that it was working

A thousand West Indian members of the RAF arrive in Britain on board a ship to give their help to the war effort. (IWM: CH 13438)

and if you weren't in war work you helped to protect. We all learned how to have a bucket of sand and how to cope with the incendiaries because they could drop like rain in your garden or on your roof. And you knew what to do with the sand and the incendiary bombs.

Myrtle Solomon was less confident:

I remember throwing sand on a bomb, for ages I kept doing exactly what I'd been told to do, and throwing this sand on and on and it just flared up again. The planes were still overhead and you thought they could see you. And that if they saw a bit of fire going up then they would drop another bomb on you, so to that extent you were petrified, but the actual incendiary ... really they were not so frightening.

The Blitz went on into the new year, and on into the early summer of 1941. Britain was still alone. In April Greece had fallen to the Germans, and a record number of British ships were sunk by U-boats in the Atlantic. At the beginning of May Liverpool was bombed every night for a week.

Some 250 miles south **Ellen Harris** was still working as a journalist in a London under siege.

I think it was May 10, and it was the night London was set afire. And I'd been in a dug-out under Liberty's in Regent Street which my father felt safe in. And I went with him. My husband was on duty in Fleet Street. And I left early enough – quite early that morning because I was to be on duty – to get home, wash and change and get back on duty in Fleet Street by eight o'clock. So this was fairly early but the raid was all finished and over. And I think I must have had to walk it – and it's a good long distance from Oxford Circus to where I lived in

on Peenemünde's rocket programme; the attack succeeds in damaging the factory, causing a major delay in the construction of V-1 flying bombs

18 NOVEMBER Berlin is attacked again by more than 400 RAF bombers dropping 1,600 tons of bombs

Islington. And I was walking over hosepipes, dozens and dozens. No bus could have run, there were hosepipes everywhere, and the firemen fighting the blazes still.

And I got to Bloomsbury and I was then walking down from Bloomsbury past Lincoln's Inn. And a man, who I learnt had been taking cover in a shelter in Lincoln's Inn Fields, middle-aged man, almost in tears, stopped me and said, 'What are we going to do? We can't go on like this, we've got to seek peace, we've got to say we must have peace. We can't go on in this way.' He was really very panicky.

A poster warns civilians to take various precautions to protect themselves against enemy air-raids before going to bed.

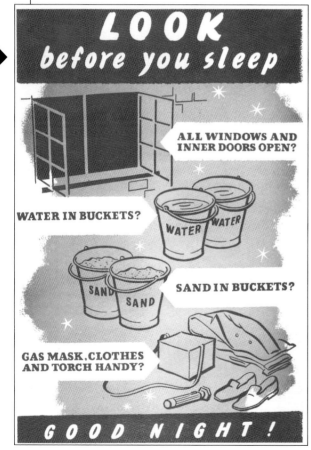

And I said to him, 'Do you realize that you're playing right into Hitler's hands? This is just what he's setting out to do. If he can do this to you, to get you into this state, and you come here and you start on me and I join in with you and I go up the road and tell somebody, and you do the same to somebody else. Now,' I said, 'you'd get people in the state of mind and their morale goes.' I said, 'What you've got to do is to remember you're in the front line as if you were in the trenches in the last war.'

I said: 'This is what I'm telling myself all the

24 NOVEMBER An entry in Goebbels's diary reveals his unhappy surprise at the way the British have been able to inflict so much bomb damage on Berlin in a single raid

28 NOVEMBER Churchill, Roosevelt and Stalin meet in Tehran to discuss the way forward against Germany; a date for the invasion of France is confirmed. Studying the film taken during a diverted photo-reconnaissance flight over Peenemünde, British

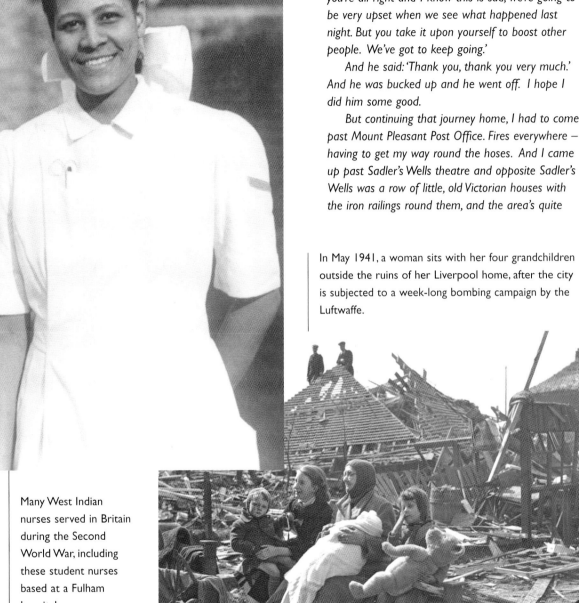

time, this is my war effort. And this is your war effort.' And I said: 'Buck up. You were under cover, you're all right and I know this is sad, we're going to be very upset when we see what happened last night. But you take it upon yourself to boost other people. We've got to keep going.'

And he said: 'Thank you, thank you very much.' And he was bucked up and he went off. I hope I did him some good.

But continuing that journey home, I had to come past Mount Pleasant Post Office. Fires everywhere – having to get my way round the hoses. And I came up past Sadler's Wells theatre and opposite Sadler's Wells was a row of little, old Victorian houses with the iron railings round them, and the area's quite

In May 1941, a woman sits with her four grandchildren outside the ruins of her Liverpool home, after the city is subjected to a week-long bombing campaign by the Luftwaffe.

Many West Indian nurses served in Britain during the Second World War, including these student nurses based at a Fulham hospital.
(IWM: PL 9609F)

intelligence discovers a similarity between constructions there, and others in northern France, which confirms that Britain will be targeted by new weapons

5 DECEMBER Acting upon information received from the photo-reconnaissance flight, raids on the V-I sites in northern France are mounted by Allied aircraft

1943

Victims of air raids sit on the streets with their belongings after their homes have been destroyed in May 1941.

As the Blitz intensified, fear of gas raids grew, and gas masks were carried at all times, but gas bombs were never used. (IWM: LD 1290)

small. Well, the whole lot – what wasn't down to the ground – had got all the insides out. And the houses opposite also had been badly blasted.

And what brought me to tears, believe it or not – first of all I saw people moving children's prams which they'd filled with little things they'd rescued from their homes, pushing the prams away, several of those, no tears, nothing whatsoever, just the firmness, 'we'll rescue what we can', they were all right; but what got me into tears was a birdcage still hanging in the window and a little, dead canary. Now can you understand that? I just burst into tears going up the road. I thought, 'This is terrible.'

My home and all around there was all right, except a main gas main, just near me, and the water mains had been hit. You couldn't have a cup

20 DECEMBER 2,000 tons of bombs are dropped on Frankfurt, Mannheim and other industrial cities in southern Germany by approximately 1,000 Allied aircraft; the V-1 sites in northern France are attacked once again

29 DECEMBER Berlin is targeted by Allied bombers for the last time this year, as RAF and USAAF forces drop 2,300 tons of bombs on the capital

11

Firemen direct their hoses on to smoking buildings in the aftermath of an air-raid in London.

of tea or anything anywhere locally. There was a local butcher man and he had some oil arrangement down in his basement. He set the stoves going. And he set up a stall outside. He cooked sausages, and whatever he'd got in his shop he cooked and he put out there for the people to come along and help themselves. Now I saw that with my own eyes. He was the butcher, he owned the place. He was a man that you wouldn't have thought was that kind of man at all. And I knew him very well to talk to and I talked to him afterwards.

'Well, poor devils,' he said, 'you know, there was no gas or water or anything. But I was able to have the stove.' And he said, 'I could cook by the oil.' He

said, 'What sort of a person would I have been?' There were a lot of rather poor people in the neighbourhood. He said, 'I just set up and they had what they wanted. I saw to it nobody took more than a meal; I sorted it out.'

I said, 'How did you charge them?'

He said, 'Oh, I didn't charge them. They couldn't even get themselves a cup of tea.'

Then I went up on duty. We were all very distressed, everything we'd seen, coming through the City and fires still raging. And I saw firemen flung across the fronts of their motors where they were so exhausted, having gone all through the night and just threw themselves across it for ten minutes' sleep. I really saw that myself.

And when it came to lunchtime, time for me to go out to lunch and it was said, 'Now, pop out and see if you can get yourself something, there's nothing

7 JANUARY Allied air raids on German flying-bomb launch sites cause delays to the deployment of the V-1s

21 JANUARY London and areas in Southern England are targeted in Hitler's retaliatory raids against Britain;

270 aircraft attack in two waves, but only 96 reach their targets and some of these are brought down. In contrast, almost 700 RAF bombers make successful raids on Berlin, Kiel and Magdeburg

1944

in the place here, there's no gas or water.' And we had a Lyons on the corner but no, they were the same. And everywhere there was not even a cup of tea. But various vans had come along. And I don't know whether it was the Salvation Army, but you could get yourself a cup of tea from these different vans. Nothing else was available anywhere.

And I went straight back. Talking about the morale of people, and just for once on that day, I think mine was going. I got back to the office and I said, 'Oh, God it's terrible.'

And I burst into tears, you see, and the editor said, 'Now, what's the matter? What is it?'

I said, 'I've just been out and the firemen are still fighting the fires and half the firemen,' I said, 'are dead on their feet. They're flinging themselves down across the engines to get ten minutes' sleep. You can't get anything anywhere to eat, you can't get a drop of water or anything outside. This is terrible.'

You know, I was looking ahead a bit, if this is now the beginning of it.

And he then – it was his turn to push morale into me – 'Now,' he said, 'you, of all people, I'm ashamed of you. You pull yourself together – we're looking to the likes of you to keep everybody going. Now,' he said, 'by tomorrow, this'll all be neat and tidy again, you'll have your water back in no time.'

I said, 'I'm not thinking of the water.'

And he gave me a jolly good lecture. 'Now,' he said, 'there's a lot of youngsters around here and they rely on you. Don't let them see you upset – they're going to be upset. So,' he said, 'keep going.'

I said, 'I'm OK, now, I'm OK, I'll be all right.' And

Using bedsheets as makeshift bags, British citizens gather as many belongings as they can carry from the remains of their ruined homes. (IWM: KY 5548 E)

27 JANUARY Berlin is raided by nearly 500 RAF bombers in bad weather; there are a number of collisions in heavy cloud

16 FEBRUARY Following another heavy bombing raid on Berlin involving 800 Allied aircraft, Goebbels overemphasizes the amount of damage sustained, in an effort to convince the Allies that the capital is no longer a crucial target

Mobile canteens provided hot drinks for those left without water and gas supplies after a damaging bombing raid.

never once after that did I falter. But it was that day, all the fires going around.

In the early days of the Blitz **Frederick Winterbotham** had been in the Whitehall bunker with Winston Churchill.

It was one raid on central London, the whole of Carlton House Terrace, just across the park from where we were, was in flames, and the bombs were dropping around. And Churchill came up smoking his cigar, and put on his tin hat, and he was in his boiler suit. And in front of the door of the underground offices was a sort of concrete screen, and everybody tried to prevent him going out in front of that because there was so much metal flying about. Not a bit. He went out and I can see him today with his hands on his stick, and smoking his cigar. We were all in a very dim light, and standing behind him, the Chiefs of Staff and Ismay and myself and my chief, and Churchill saying, 'My God, we'll get the buggers for this.'

18 FEBRUARY London is targeted by the Luftwaffe in an air raid involving 187 aircraft dropping incendiary bombs

19 FEBRUARY RAF Bomber Command loses 78 aircraft from a total of 730 when night-fighters and anti-aircraft fire decimate a raid on Leipzig

1944

CHAPTER ELEVEN

DISTANT THUNDER

BRITAIN DID NOT WIN THE BLITZ. IT SURVIVED IT, but many people did not. In 1940 and 1941 more than 42,000 civilians were killed in the bombing. The centres of many cities and towns were reduced to rubble, some local administrations collapsed, those who could get out, got out. There was cowardice and chaos and selflessness and heroism.

On 10 May 1941 the London Blitz reached an horrific crescendo. Nearly 1,500 people died, nearly 2,000 were seriously injured.

Worse was expected. It never came – to Britain. General Albert Kesselring's Luftflotte Two, which had flown through the Battle of Britain and devastated Coventry and southern England in the Blitz, had gone elsewhere. So had General Gerd von Rundstedt, victor in the Fall of France, and the tank general, Heinz Guderian, whose forces had cut France in half. They had gone to prepare for Operation Barbarossa, the invasion of the Soviet Union on 22 June 1941.

His own espionage network warned the Soviet dictator Joseph Stalin; the Americans, thanks to a German anti-Nazi, warned him, and so did the British, relying on their intelligence network, and Ultra, Hut Three at Bletchley.

Frederick Winterbotham:
We knew to the day when the invasion was going to take place and we knew where most of the German forces were. Somebody used to make up a report, which was handed to the Russian mission, giving an outline of what we knew, but in no case giving away that we got it from intercepted material. It was a summary of the information which we would have had from other sources, and telling the Russians

Joseph Stalin, Soviet dictator, who dismissed the immediate risk of a Nazi attack on the Soviet Union before Operation Barbarossa in June 1941.

A surprise aerial attack on the US naval base at Pearl Harbor by the Japanese on 7 December 1941 brings the US into the war.

what the Germans were trying to do. I don't think they believed a word of it. I suppose over the time they found that we were generally correct.

The raids on Britain did not stop. Hull was heavily bombed that summer, Newcastle upon Tyne raided that September. And Luftwaffe fighter-bombers mounted hit-and-run raids across the south. But with Barbarossa the airborne assault on the British Isles gradually faded away. Then, on 7 December 1941 the Japanese attack on Pearl Harbor brought the United States into the war. Isolation was over.

On 23 February 1942 Sir Arthur Harris became chief of the RAF's Bomber Command. The Luftwaffe's attacks on Britain had failed to seriously impede British production, or to break morale. But Bomber Command's daylight attacks on Germany had been costly and ineffectual and its night-time raids inaccurate. The RAF developed new navigational aids, and, in mid-March 1942, Harris sent more than 200 bombers to the industrial town of Essen, site of a Krupp armaments factory. It was not a success. At the end of that month the medieval, Hanseatic League city of Lübeck was hit by 191 bombers dropping incendiaries. Half of the port was destroyed.

The Baedeker guidebooks had been the way that peacetime travellers had found their way around the glories of European civilization. Less than a month after Lübeck came the first Baedeker Raid, as Hitler sought vengeance with attacks on towns like York, Norwich, and Canterbury.

Vera Howard was a fourteen-year-old in Exeter, whose experience of the Blitz had been limited to meetings with London evacuees. On 24 April 1942 a couple of dozen Luftwaffe bombers hit the city.

> *I had just left school and I was working in a store in the centre. Now, we were not allowed to go into the city for several days. I tried to get work, you see, and when I did go up, as far as where I did work, which was the St Thomas's end of Exeter, I just couldn't believe it. There was a lot of damage done by the incendiaries. It was more burnt than bombed.*

In the next forty months high explosives, but particularly incendiaries, devoured the cities, churches, factories, shrines and people of the Axis powers. The Blitz on Britain had been terrible. The response – sustained area bombing – was horrific.

In 1944 twenty-four-year-old **Petrea Grant** – who was to marry Frederick Winterbotham in 1947 – was a plotter at Fighter Command's operations room at

The great Krupp munitions works at Essen, pictured prior to RAF bombing raids.

30 MARCH During an unsuccessful raid on Nuremberg in which only a small area of the target is hit accurately by 2,500 bombs, the RAF suffers the largest number of aircraft and aircrew lost in a single raid, as 96 aircraft from a total of 795 are shot down by night-fighters

York is bombed in the first Baedeker raid; the railway station suffers major bomb damage.

A young sergeant pilot works out a course for a future mission in the navigation room. (IWM: CH 7466)

Bentley Priory in Stanmore. Her brother, aged twenty, was a bomber pilot.

He did, I think, over one and a half tours and he was going out on the big raids, Emden, Kiel, Cologne, those terrible ones. That was pretty ghastly because I obviously kept an eye on the place he flew from – he was at Medmenham – for a time so when you saw a lot of flights of bombers going out you were a little inclined to wait until they all got back.

18 APRIL In the heaviest Allied air raid of the war over 2,000 bombers drop more than 4,000 tons of bombs on Germany. Meanwhile, the last of the

Operation Steinbeck raids occurs over London, with an attack on the capital by more than 100 bombers from Luftflotte 9.

1944

In 1942 **Reginald Lewis**, aged twenty, was a navigator.

The Ruhr, of all targets, was, I always thought, the most awe inspiring, because if you happened to be bombing somewhere like Essen, which really was in the centre of the Ruhr area, a very heavily defended area, one had probably something like ten minutes, a quarter of an hour – maybe twenty minutes – of flying through a fairly rough area, inasmuch as flak was bursting all over the place; not necessarily being fired at us, but it was bursting all over the place. There were certainly hundreds of searchlights in the sky, one could see other aircraft, coned in the searchlights, being shot at. One could see aircraft going down in flames and it was, all in all, I would almost say, a frightening experience. Certainly exciting as a first entry into battle. And one was very grateful to get home, really.

Many did not. More than 57,000 Bomber Command aircrew died in the raids on Germany. On 30 May 1942 Bomber

Canterbury is badly hit in the Baedeker Raids; many families are made homeless in 1942.

Sir Arthur Harris earned the press title 'Bomber Harris' as Commander-in-Chief of RAF Bomber Command.

24 APRIL A raid on Munich by RAF Bomber Command is achieved by an approach through Swiss air space, avoiding the German air-warning system

12 MAY According to German Armaments Minister Albert Speer, the Allied bombing of synthetic fuel plants at four sites in Germany threatens an end to armaments production in Germany

6 JUNE D-Day landings – Allied troops invade Europe, storming the beaches of Normandy, France

13 JUNE The first V-1 flying bombs are launched at England from the Pas-de-Calais; only four out of ten bombs cross the English Channel successfully, but six people are killed in Bethnal Green

1944

Ground crew roll out bombs from a bomb dump in preparation for an attack on German targets.
(IWM: CH 14533)

Command launched its first 1,000-plane raid on Cologne. A year later, from 24 July to 2 August 1943 Bomber Command, and the US Army Air Force, carried out Operation Gomorrah on Hamburg. On July 28 the fires the RAF started coalesced into a 150mph firestorm sucking in oxygen, raising temperatures to more than 1400 degrees and killing, that night, more than 40,000 people.

Myrtle Solomon:
When I realized the quantities of material we were dropping on Germany – and we were told it was very much more than what they'd dropped on us – I thought, 'How terrifying it must be.'

The Allied bombing aroused criticism at the time in Britain. Bomber Command's chaplain Canon John Collins, asked whether the issue was 'the ethics of bombing' or 'the bombing of ethics'.

Hamburg is in ruins following the sustained bombing attack by Allied aircraft which is Operation Gomorrah.

14 JUNE A flying bomb is chased and shot down over the English Channel by an RAF Mosquito, the first V-1 to be destroyed in this way

15 JUNE Areas along the south coast of England are strongly protected against German flying bombs by anti-aircraft defences both on the ground and in the air

1944

The pilot and co-pilot of a Wellington bomber prior to departing for a raid on enemy territory.
(IWM: D 4737)

A Lancaster bomber is silhouetted amid flares, smoke and flak during a Bomber Command attack on Hamburg at the end of July 1943.
(IWM: C 3371)

21 JUNE RAF fighters plan successful bombing missions against V-1 rocket-launching ramps in France, as well as chasing and destroying many more flying bombs in mid-flight

4 JULY The RAF's 617 Squadron (the 'Dambusters') carry out bombing raids on limestone caves 30 miles north west of Paris, used to store V-1 bombs; the caves remain intact

1944

CHAPTER TWELVE

VENGEANCE

EARLY IN 1944 THE LUFTWAFFE RETURNED TO Britain. In January the 'Little Blitz' hit London and South Wales, Hull and Bristol, but by April the raids were petering out. Anticipation was mounting about an Allied invasion of France, but amidst that excitement there were other rumours, about new, terrifying German weapons.

By the early summer **Rosemary Horstmann** was based at Bletchley's Hut Three.

What the Germans were doing in 1944 – which we got the beginning of at Bletchley – was they were beginning to use jet aircraft. They were tremendously excited at the possibilities that jet aircraft would offer and there was one squadron, one group – I think it

Two German V-1 flying bombs are illustrated in flight, heading for targets in Britain.

A V-1 flying bomb is loaded on to a launch pad.

Illustration of a V-2 rocket, 'Vergeltungswaffe', the first long-range ballistic missile, which carried a one-tonne warhead delivered at a speed of 5000 kph.

was KG65 – which were re-equipped with Me 262s which were the first (fully operational) German jet aircraft and we, I think, on the Allied side, we were quite apprehensive as to what they could do and used to spend a lot of time being absolutely sure where that group was. They used to move between an aerodrome in south Germany and an aerodrome in north Germany. We were always very carefully tracking down exactly where they were located.

The manned jet aircraft were never a threat. Their only appearance over the British Isles was when Arado 234 bombers flew reconnaissance missions to East Anglia. They

RAF aerial reconnaissance view of the German research station at Peenemünde, where V-2 rocket tests took place.

A V-2 rocket targeted for southern England takes off. The Allies had no defence against it.

6 JULY Churchill informs Parliament that 2,752 civilians have been killed as a result of attacks by 3,745 V-1 flying bombs

11 JULY Over a million children are evacuated from London to safer rural areas following the mass destruction caused by the V-1 bombs

flew so high, so fast, that their presence went undiscovered until after the war.

But there was a threat. The Vergeltungswaffen reprisal weapons; these were the V-2 rocket, and the V-1 flying bomb, the 'Doodlebug'.

Frederick Winterbotham at Bletchley was tracking the Germans' work on them.

We'd heard quite a bit about their experiments on Rugen Island and up at Peenemünde up in the Baltic. And now we were getting reports from agents in France with the exact positions of where these things were being put. At first, of course, nobody knew precisely what these strange launching pads were, with these long sort of shoots where the thing was shot off into the air. And we got a lot of funny descriptions of drainpipes being laid with rails on top of them and that sort of thing. However, we did get to know exactly what the V-1 was like and probably what damage it could do. There were photographs taken over Peenemünde and the whole thing was thoroughly investigated.

It was investigated, but despite massive bombing of the launch sites, V-1 attacks could not be prevented. On 6 June 1944 the Allied armies landed in Normandy. A week later a Luftwaffe spotter plane was detailed to fly to London and observe the arrival of the first V-1s. The plane was shot down in east London. But soon after 4 a.m. the first V-1 hit Swanscombe in Kent; more hits followed that day at Cuckfield, Sevenoaks and Bethnal Green in London's East End, where six people were killed.

British air defence had the problem that a shot-down V-1 might explode on a built-up area; the aim was to bring them down away from towns. The key weapons were anti-aircraft guns, barrage balloons and aircraft, but the pulse-jet-powered V-1 was fast, with a top speed of more than 400 m.p.h. Between 15 and 16 June the Germans launched 244 V-1s,

19 JULY Anti-aircraft batteries on the south-east coast of England start to use proximity-fused shells designed to explode when a nearby target is sensed; consequently V-1 bombs become easier to destroy by ground fire

2 AUGUST The highest number of V-1 bombs to be launched in a single day are targeted at London; from a total of 316, more than 100 reach the capital, causing damage to Tower Bridge, and to armaments factories on the outskirts of London

1944

of which 144 actually entered southern England.

Roland Beamont had moved on from the Hurricanes of the Battle of Britain, and was now commanding a wing of Hawker Tempest V fighters.

Two Canadian soldiers sit on a V-1 bomb that failed to reach its intended target.

On June 16 we were alerted – by noises like a motorbike going through the night sky, which were the first of these V-1s – to stand by with a whole wing at dawn, and from dawn on that day we were totally engaged in defence against V-1s with the Tempest. In action these proved to be the fastest fighter by a long margin at that level, and the most capable one because we had a very good gun platform with the aeroplane. It could fire its 20mm cannon very accurately.

We were able to shoot down a great number of the things in the first few weeks, to such an extent

that 11 Group asked me to provide a recommendation for certain ways of improving this defensive action, which I did. As a result, an area along the south coast, from Eastbourne to Dover, was restricted for our purposes to Tempests and a squadron of the fastest Spitfires, which were Spitfire XIVs, and a wing of Mustang P51s, which were again faster than anything else. All other fighter aeroplanes, all other types and the slower marques of Spitfire were kept out of that area and we were able to concentrate on it. In the period from June 16 to the end of July the Newchurch Tempest wing shot down over 600 V-1s.

1944

25 AUGUST Paris is liberated by the Allied troops

27 AUGUST RAF Bomber Command launches its first major daylight bombing raid on Germany since the early war months

A Hawker Tempest V fighter, used to shoot down the vast numbers of V-1 rockets sent to hit urban Britain.
(IWM: E (MOS)1355)

The German Messerschmitt 262A-1 – the first German jet fighter aircraft – capable of reaching top speeds of 530 m.p.h., over 100 m.p.h. faster than conventional Allied fighters.

6 SEPTEMBER In response to the progress being made by the Allies in Europe, blackout rules in Britain are relaxed and the training of Home Guard units comes to an end

8 SEPTEMBER The first V-2 rocket lands in Chiswick, London, killing three and injuring ten; fired from a mobile launcher in the German-occupied suburb of The Hague, the rocket's 192-mile journey takes only 5 minutes

1944

Hitler insisted that the V-1 should have one target – London. Thus a 2,000-year-old city, established by the Romans, became the primary target of a weapon that hinted at a dreadful future for humanity. The British shifted their forward defences closer to the coast as a V-1 'bomb alley' opened up in Kent and Sussex. A new wave of evacuation swept over a grey and cloudy summer city.

By early September, when General Bernard Montgomery's 2nd Army overran V-1 launch sites in the Pas de Calais, nearly

Viewed from a Fleet Street roof-top, a flying bomb is seen falling in Central London; it landed in a side road off Drury Lane. (IWM: HU 636)

7,000 V-1s had crossed the English coast. Someone who had seen plenty of them was Londoner **Ellen Harris**.

The doodlebugs used to go through the air like a huge bullet, but very, very big. And you'd see it go through the sky with a flame out the back. And I remember the first one I saw. Standing in the

4 OCTOBER Germany's Me 262, its first jet aircraft to fly in combat, is sent into action for the first time, a day after its official deployment as a fighter

13 OCTOBER In an effort to prevent its use by the Allies, the Germans fire V-1 and V-2 bombs against the port of Antwerp

middle of the road and pointing, I said, 'Look, it's a doodlebug.' The reason being, being in the press, we knew these things were coming. And we'd hear people talk about the first one – it went far out in the east and everybody was talking about the damage it had done. Well, we knew what it was but we had to keep very quiet. So of course when the next was coming our way, we knew what to expect. And they were pretty awful.

Later I'd just got opposite the Houses of Parliament and a doodlebug went over our heads, and everybody was now making for the Westminster station. Whitehall was going home as well, so there were big crowds around. So this doodlebug was going overhead – and I, inside, was terrified. But I wouldn't turn a hair – would I run? No fear! Nobody else was running, I wasn't going to run. But I looked

for the first person who would throw himself down in the gutter, and I'd have followed – but not one. And this doodlebug went over and exploded over Green Park, which is only down the road. And everybody calmly walked to their station as if nothing was happening.

One Sunday afternoon I remember my sister-in-law had called. It was one of the old Victorian houses and the kitchen was a converted conservatory, which meant a lot of glass. Now, the warning had gone and all was very quiet for a long time, we'd almost

A V-2 rocket causes major destruction in Smithfield Market, London; a badly injured woman is carried to safety on a stretcher by a policeman, civilian and two rescue workers. (IWM: HU 65896)

30 OCTOBER RAF Bomber Command launches a two-night bombing raid on Cologne, dropping more than 6,300 tons of bombs

8 NOVEMBER Churchill informs the public that Germany's V-2 rocket campaign is the cause of the explosions across south-east England. The supersonic rocket drops from a great height, giving no warning of its approach, unlike aircraft and V-1s

1944

forgotten it. And then we heard this thing approaching and we heard it go over. And both of us shouted, 'Down!' And we were both flat on the floor, it seemed to have come suddenly. And it went over us and went on. And there was a most unholy bang. As the crow flies, it wasn't a great distance away.

Very shortly after, I thought, 'I wonder how Dad is' – my father lived not far away. And the direction it seemed to go was right over – although I knew it had gone over further. And we met halfway. I was flying down to him and he was coming up to me. And he was covered with plaster, although the thing hadn't gone off near him at all. But it had shaken everything so badly. The plaster came down on him.

And: 'Are you all right?' – both of us, you see. 'Yes, all right.'

We had a little chat.

And, not then – I think it was a few days afterwards – I went down into the vicinity and walked round purposely. I'd been told where this had fallen. And it wasn't one or two houses; it was the whole street of houses, both sides. This was an unknown enemy. You only heard him approach. You only knew that he was on his way, you didn't know which way.

They were more frightening than the bombs. You seemed to know what was coming with the planes. But we were in a particularly nasty place. They came across Kent – I was almost central London, you see.

An RAF flight of Mustang P51s, also highly effective in the destruction of V-1 bombs. (IWM: CNA 3490)

25 NOVEMBER A V-2 rocket lands on a Woolworth's store in Deptford, south London, killing 160 people

27 NOVEMBER The RAF makes use of the 12,000lb Tallboy bomb for the first time on a German city in a raid on Munich, causing damage and destruction to more than 600 buildings

Just a mile down the road was Mansion House and Bank – don't think more than a mile. They came across Kent that way and they also came in across the other way from the south-east and they all seemed to be making for London proper and we used to get both lots. So it was very unpleasant for some time. The Blitz was nasty but you felt you were doing something. You felt you were fighting it off. You were doing something, but with the doodlebugs and the rockets you knew there was nothing that you could do.

In the summer of 1944 the artist – and war artist – twenty-eight-year-old **Eleanor Hudson** had another job, that of supplying tea from canteen lorry to V-1-blitzed west London.

I was asked to help because I could drive, at a centre in Notting Hill Gate, when flying bombs began. They had a fleet of converted laundry vans so I was driving this great gigantic laundry van, very high, an old-fashioned thing. I could be called at any time of day and night really, if any incident happened, and many flying bombs were coming down, all the time, so you could do two or three shifts continuously. It was very exhausting.

From where I lived in Earls Court I had to take a bicycle, and bicycle madly uphill to Notting Hill Gate in the middle of the night, perhaps, and jump into my laundry van, with a helper, and our great urns of tea and sandwiches, and then I'd come out tearing down Church Street Kensington.

In the daytime there was a policeman. Even if it was war, there was a policeman, who used to grin when he saw me coming and stop the traffic and signal me on, but it was very strange because I had no horn on this van. It used to worry me that I couldn't blow a horn for safety. So one day I was lying back yawning, and having one moment's rest, and suddenly up there over my head, straight above me was an old-fashioned rubber bulb horn and I was delighted to find that. So next time I went tearing down Church Street I reached up and made a sort of 'toot-toot' at the policeman who really fell

over. He was so astonished.

There was a very nasty bomb that came down at the corner of Earls Court Road and Kensington High Street, when a whole block of flats called Troy Court were half destroyed, with many people in a restaurant there. And also a Lyons Corner house on the other corner, and we were working away giving quick half-cups of tea to the choked men who were digging in all this fog of dust, and suddenly a young American soldier came running in and jumped into the back of our van and said, 'Oh ma'am, please let me help, let me wash up the cups.'

He was very white and so he insisted, so we handed over this quick washing-up that was going on. And after a while his colour improved and then he said, 'It was a great shock to me when this happened and I ran into the building and by the time I had taken out so many dead people I was sick, I felt terrible, and then I saw your little kitchen and I jumped in. It felt like home. I thought this is the nearest to having my mum. If I can help here and do some washing up.'

And so we were very touched and helped him on his way.

The V-1 seemed to sum up the impersonality of death technology, one step beyond the bombers of 1940–41, or the Lancasters and Flying Fortresses that droned day and night towards Germany. Even after their launching areas were overrun, the attacks – more than 10,000 in total – continued with around 1,600 launches from aircraft, which hit as far north as Manchester, Oldham and Hull, and as far west as Shropshire. Southampton, key invasion port, devastated in 1940–41 was also a V-1 target. But there was more. On 8 September 1944, Chiswick and Epping were rocked by huge explosions, preceded by sonic booms.

In the months leading up to the end of the war in Europe more than 1,300 V-2 ballistic rockets, reaching speeds of 3,000 m.p.h. were

3 DECEMBER The Home Guard, Britain's auxiliary army, is disbanded after providing service to the war effort since 1940

4 DECEMBER The Germans opt to limit V-2 launches to night-time, prompted by an RAF air raid on a number of rocket-launch sites

1944

fired at London, and a further 44 at Norwich and Ipswich. Less than half hit their targets, but at the cost of 2,724 lives.

Rosamond Boddy was a young land girl who had returned to work in London in 1944.

The V-2s were just a sort of bang and the floor rocked a bit. If you heard the bang you knew you were all right. You didn't hear anything before so you couldn't spend your life wondering if you were going to hear a bang, so one tried not to think about anything until they went off. So that was all right.

Not everybody agreed. And as victory approached, exhaustion swept over a capital, and a country of bombsites, wrecked houses and rationing. **Myrtle Solomon** was a civil servant.

I remember feeling more and more weary. I also remember, in London, I think we all became more frightened, and fear, I think, is catching. And the doodlebugs were pretty frightening, but the V-2s were terrifying. And I don't know whether we were tired by then, or what it was, but a lot of people would admit to that – that we were much more scared then than when the bombs were raining down on us during the Blitz. I think we were tired. I was only longing for the end by then.

As the Allied armies advanced, the threat of the V weapons ended, but the full horror was just unfolding. The V-2 had been developed by a group of Nazi scientists led by Wernher von Braun who, in 1945, was the central figure in that group spirited by the United States government to its New Mexico-based rocket programme. A decade later he was a cleansed, all-American citizen and, with the 1969 moon landing, a national hero. But the V-2 on which his triumphs were based was primarily produced by slave labourers at Nordhausen, at what was labelled 'Dora', a complex of galleries and tunnels inside the

Kohnstein Hill in the Harz Mountains.

News Chronicle reporter **Stanley Baron** had moved on from the London Blitz of 1940, accompanying the Allied advance into Germany. Then he arrived at Dora . . .

Nordhausen was a dreadful place. In some ways I regard it as being almost worse – not in scale but in spirit – than Belsen or these other ghastly places. You went into the mouth of a great cave. And inside the cave there were some thirty or forty miles of tunnels. It was the largest underground factory in Europe. And it was there that they were building the V-1s and the V-2.

Going into the cave I was aware of a number of strange emaciated figures who appeared to be wearing pyjamas. I realized afterwards that of course this was the uniform of the prisoners. We went first of all into the works. And there we saw every sign of sophisticated engineering, of man at his scientifically most brilliant. And then I came out again. And this time we went to the quarters of the slave labour. And we saw men dying while we watched. I remember in one particular dark corner waving my torch around, just seeing the glint of eyes and very weak voices tried to explain who they were.

I would say virtually the whole of the work force there consisted of political prisoners of the Germans. It was estimated afterwards that something like 20,000 Poles had died there. And when I say that spiritually it was almost the worst possible place – it was not even governed by the mad theory of race that Belsen was governed by. These people were not being destroyed because of their race, because they were Jews or because they were gypsies. They were being used as – and destroyed in the process – they were being used as material for this vast scientific apparatus that was producing weapons of war destined for London.

And the contrast between that of highly advanced technical ability of the Germans and what they were able to do to ordinary humanity was so great that this has struck me always as being a really most

16 DECEMBER In the Ardennes the Battle of the Bulge, a last-ditch attempt by the Germans to divide the Allied thrust towards Germany, begins

24 DECEMBER Manchester is hit by V-1 bombs launched from Heinkel He-111s; the city centre is hit by a single bomb, while the rest fall in the outskirts

extraordinary example, I suppose, of the dichotomy which can exist in the human mind. It was terrible, absolutely terrible ... and we saw men dying while we watched.

Inmates of the Lager-Nordhausen camp; in horrific conditions prisoners were subjected to slave labour in the underground factory where V-1 and V-2 bombs were constructed.

22 JANUARY Spitfires bomb and destroy the Dutch factory responsible for the manufacture of liquid oxygen, used to fuel V-2 rockets

4 FEBRUARY Yalta Conference – Churchill, Roosevelt and Stalin meet once again to discuss the world's post-war future

1945

CHAPTER THIRTEEN

LATE SPRING

On 30 April 1945, Adolf Hitler, the man who had unleashed barbarism, committed suicide. On 7 May, the German High Command surrendered. May 8 was declared Victory in Europe, VE, Day.

Ellen Harris was in the House of Commons.

I shall never forget it. I couldn't move, I couldn't do anything, whatever had happened. Although we'd known this was coming, the House itself just went into one great roar of cheers, papers went up in the air, I just sat and the tears were rolling down. And there was nothing I could do about that – but it was relief, you see, after all this long time. And this kept up, the roaring and cheering and shouting, for some time. And then the Speaker dissolved the House.

Prime Minister Winston Churchill waves to crowds gathered in Whitehall on VE Day.

VE-Day celebrations: the national press reports on the jubilant British nation following Victory in Europe.

Daily Mail

VICTORY EDITION

NO. 15,290 ONE PENNY * FOR KING AND EMPIRE TUESDAY, MAY 8, 1945

3-POWER ANNOUNCEMENT TO-DAY; BUT BRITAIN KNEW LAST NIGHT

VE-DAY—IT'S ALL OVER

All quiet till 9 p.m.—then the London crowds went mad in the West End

THE Face of Victory—by day and night: Roadways in and around Piccadilly-circus were jammed nearly solid yesterday afternoon by crowds waiting to hear VE-Day announced. Then they decided not to wait—they began to celebrate. These Daily Mail pictures give you a vivid impression of the great concourse of joy—above by day; on the left, by night. Other scenes—Pages THREE and FOUR.

PM put off the big speech

UNTIL TO-DAY

By **WILSON BROADBENT,**
Diplomatic Correspondent

GERMANY surrendered unconditionally to the Allies yesterday. But there will be no official announcement of victory until 3 p.m. to-day—officially described as VE-Day—when Mr. Churchill will give the news to the world.

He will follow this with an address to the House of Commons, and at 9 p.m. the King will speak to Britain and the Empire.

Mr. Churchill's private room at the House of Commons was last night "wired-up" so that if he wishes he can make his broadcast from there.

To-day's announcement will be made simultaneously in London, Washington, and Moscow. To-day, therefore, is the first of the promised two-days V-holiday for the country.

Broadcasts will also be made by General Eisenhower and Field Marshals Montgomery and Alexander.

Mr. Churchill's two statements to-day will not affect his intention to broadcast at length on Thursday night, the fifth anniversary of his assumption of the Premiership.

After his statement in the House of Commons, Mr. Churchill will propose the adjournment of business while M.P.s attend a special Service of Thanksgiving at St. Margaret's Church, Westminster. They will then return to the House of Commons, adjourn, and arrange to meet again on Wednesday.

Until shortly before 6 o'clock last night it was fully expected that Mr. Churchill would be able to announce the news that the war was over.

Victory lunch

He had been standing by the microphone from some time after 3 o'clock, and everything was ready for him to break into the normal programmes of the B.B.C.

Earlier in the day he had been speaking on the Transatlantic telephone to Washington, and he also had several calls to Moscow. His object was to obtain an agreed time for releasing the big news.

There had been a previous agreement that there should be simultaneous times for release. Apparently in London it was understood that Monday would be suitable to all concerned.

In anticipation of this important occasion, Mr. Churchill gave a special Victory luncheon party at No. 10, Downing-street, for the Chiefs of Staff, whose health he personally proposed.

After luncheon Mr. Churchill was ready to broadcast, but no news of Washington's or Moscow's assent had been received.

It was nearly 6 o'clock when it was learned that both the United States and the Soviet Government were in favour of postponing the formal announcing until this afternoon.

Moscow preferred this course because of certain final formalities connected with the German surrender, which will take place to-day. Washington had other reasons which are not yet known. So Mr. Churchill, finding himself in a minority, had to agree.

TRUMAN, DE GAULLE SPEAK TO-DAY

President Truman and General de Gaulle, like Mr. Churchill, are to speak to their respective nations over the radio at 3 p.m. to-day.

TARAKAN NEARLY CUT IN TWO

Manila, Tuesday.—Allies cleared ground east of the main oilfield on Tarakan, off Borneo, and advanced across the island to within a mile and a half of the east shore. Fighting continues for Tarakan town.—B.U.P.

U.S. made it VE-Day all the same

Work walk-out

From **DON IDDON,**
Daily Mail Correspondent

NEW YORK, Monday.

THIS was VE-Day in the U.S.—official or not.

The celebrations began in New York at breakfast-time, a few minutes after word came from Rheims, France, that Germany had surrendered unconditionally to Britain, the United States, and Russia.

They went on all day despite an avalanche of confused messages, lack of official confirmation, half-denials, and a barrage of rumours that the surrender was a hoax.

The American public, and particularly the New York public, this time was determined that this was the end of the war in Europe, and resolved to commemorate it.

The first reaction, and it was the same all over Manhattan, was to jab open windows, tear up telephone directories, and hurl paper into the streets.

For hours tons upon tons of ticker tape, torn-up newspapers, envelopes, letters, magazines, and in some instances hats and waste-paper baskets, cascaded down.

Jammed roads

Tens of thousands of people abandoned work and rushed into the Times-square area, shouting and singing. Motorists blew their hooters, factory whistles shrieked, and in New York Bay ships sounded their sirens.

Bands of Service men and girls paraded the avenues, waving flags, shouting and yelling, planting kisses on strangers, cavorting in and out of bars.

Great stores, offices, the banks, the factories closed down as staffs walked out *en masse*.

Traffic was completely tied up in mid-town as throngs of gesticulating, laughing people jammed roadways, jumped on to the running-boards of private cars, taxis, and buses.

At first city officials, led by Mayor La Guardia attempted to curb the jubilation.

Over the radio came a reminder that there was nothing official, that it was merely a report which had declared that war in Europe was over. The people ignored the advice.

Daily Mail

IN accordance with the expressed desire of the Government that workers generally should enjoy a day's holiday following the announcement of the cessation of hostilities in Europe, The Daily Mail, in common with other London morning newspapers, will not be pub-

SYMBOL of the mood of London, this man, at the top of a lamp-post, waves a flag above the crowds.—Daily Mail picture.

The war still goes on here—

PRAGUE BOMBED AS SS SHOOT CZECH CIVILIANS

GERMAN bombs are falling on Prague for the first time as the war in Europe enters its last hours. In defiance of surrender orders, German forces in Czecho-Slovakia are fighting on. They are venting their last spite on the Czechs, shooting them down ruthlessly in the streets of the capital.

Refugees from Prague who have reached Allied-occupied Pilsen say that, in many cases, the S.S. went through the city driving people out of their houses into the streets.

And there other S.S. men mowed them down with machine-guns. The S.S., according to the refugees, know they will probably be executed when caught and have abandoned all normal conduct.

That the S.S. are completely out of hand is indicated in a broadcast by the German commander in Bohemia and Moravia warning his troops to respect international law.

Two columns of General Patton's tanks are racing to Prague's rescue and were last reported seven miles

A Czech Spitfire squadron and formations of large aircraft carrying Czech ground troops, have left Britain for Czecho-Slovakia.

Broadcasting from London last night, Dr. Hubert Ripka, Czecho-Slovak Minister of Foreign Trade, said that, by fighting on after the general capitulation, the Germans had placed themselves beyond the law and would be dealt with as saboteurs.

Pilsen kisses

PILSEN, Monday.

LIEUT.-GENERAL MAJEWLSKI, commanding the German gar-

BACK PAGE—Col. EIGHT

Piccadilly's bonfires started a 'chain'

By **GUY RAMSEY**

LONDON, dead from six until nine, suddenly broke into victory life last night. Suddenly, spontaneously, deliriously. The people of London, denied VE-Day officially, held their own jubilation. "VE-Day may be to-morrow," they said, "but the war is over to-night." Bonfires blazed from Piccadilly to Wapping.

The sky once lit by the glare of the blitz shone red with the Victory glow. The last trains departed from the West End unregarded. The pent-up spirits of the throng, the polyglot throng that is London in war-time, burst out, and by 11 o'clock the capital was ablaze with enthusiasm.

Processions formed up out of nowhere, disintegrating for no reason, to re-form somewhere else. Waving flags, marching in step, with linked arms or half-embraced, the people strode down the great thoroughfares—Piccadilly, Regent-street, the Mall, to the portals of Buckingham Palace.

They marched and counter-marched so as not to get too far from the centre. And from them, in harmony and discord, rose song. The songs of the last war, the songs of a century ago. The songs of the beginning of this war—"Roll out the Barrel" and "Tipperary"; "Ilkla Moor" and "Loch Lomond"; "Bless 'em All" and "Pack Up Your Troubles."

ROCKETS AND SONGS

Rockets—found no-one knows where, set-off by no-one knows whom—streaked into the sky, exploding not in death but a burst of scarlet fire. A pile of straw filled with thunder-flashes salvaged from some military dump spurted and exploded near Leicester-square.

Every car that challenged the milling, moiling throng was submerged in humanity. They climbed on the running-boards, on the bonnet, on the roof. They hammered on the panels. They shouted and sang.

Against the drumming on metal came the clash of cymbals, improvised out of dustbin lids. The dustbin itself was a football for an impromptu Rugger scrum. Bubbling, exploding with gaiety, the people "mafficked." Headlights silhouetted couples kissing, couples cheering, couples waving flags.

Every cornice, every lamp-post was scaled. Americans marched with A.T.S., girls in civvies, fresh from their work benches, ran by the side of battle-dressed

Continued in Back Page, Col. 3

SCHACHT SAVED BY 'FIFTH'

Niemoller, too

Daily Mail Special Correspondent

ALLIED H.Q., Italy, Monday.

SOME of the most famous victims of Nazi-ism have been rescued by the Fifth Army from the Prager Wildsee prison camp, near Obbiaco, Italy.

Among them was **Pastor Niemoller**, head of the German Confessional Church, whose defiance of Hitler led to a seven years' incarceration in concentration camps.

A few hours after his release Pastor Niemoller held a service in the lounge of a hotel.

His text was the words of Isaiah:

For the mountains shall depart, and the hills be removed; but my kindness shall not depart from thee, neither shall the covenant of my peace be removed, saith the Lord that hath mercy on thee.

In all, the Fifth Army saved 129 hostages, including **Dr. Schuschnigg**, former Chancellor of Austria, who during the week-end was erroneously reported to have been executed.

Dr. Schuschnigg's wife was also found. **M. Leon Blum**, former Socialist Premier of France, and his wife, were also freed.

'Evil Hitler'

The camp in which these famous people were found was a smallish affair—a group of huts around a chateau on a hillside. But behind its barbed wire the Fifth Army men found many high officers—Greek, Russian, Hungarian—and a number of Germans including **Dr. Schacht**, former German Minister of Finance and President of the Reichsbank.

Asked if Hitler was sane, Dr. Schacht said: "In some things no, in others he is a genius."

Someone suggested an evil genius, and Schacht said: "Yes, an evil genius . . . an evil and diabolical genius."

VE-WEATHER

Strait of Dover yesterday: Victory weather, with hours of sun-

GOEBBELS' BODY IN A SHELTER

GOEBBELS, the German Propaganda Minister, his wife, and five children have been found dead in Berlin.

Moscow says that their bodies were found in an air-raid shelter near the Reichstag, and it has been established that all died of poisoning.

No trace has been found of the bodies of Hitler or Göring.

There was speculation in London last night whether the Nazi leaders may have fled to a place of hiding.

It was pointed out, however, that their bodies may have been destroyed in the wreckage of the burning Chancellery or some other building.

MONTY MEETS ROKOSSOVSKY

4 toasts at lunch

TWENTY-FIRST ARMY GROUP, Monday.—Field-Marshal Montgomery lunched to-day with Marshal Konstantin Rokossovsky at Wismar.

It was their first meeting, and very cordial greetings were exchanged.

Toasts were drunk to the Allied armies, Mr. Churchill, Marshal Stalin, and President Truman.—*Reuter.*

Lord Lascelles at the Palace

The King's nephew, Lord Lascelles, and the Queen's nephew, the Master of Elphinstone, recently freed from a German prisoners' camp, arrived in London yesterday by plane.

They drove from the airfield to Buckingham Palace, where they were welcomed home by the King and Queen and Princess Elizabeth

ARRESTED POLES MAY BE TRIED BY LUBLIN

LUBLIN radio said yesterday that the Polish Provisional Government may demand that General Okulicki and others of the 16 Poles arrested by the Russians be tried both in Warsaw and Moscow for high treason.

The radio said: "Public opinion in Poland has received with indignation the news of the action of Okulicki and his accomplices, who are accused of carrying out diversionary activities against the Red Army.

"Because the criminal activities of Okulicki and his accomplices were also directed against the re-born Polish State, it constitutes high treason.

"The Provisional Government reserves the right to demand that Okulicki and his accomplices be turned over to the Polish authorities to be indicted in the courts of the Republic as well."

M. Mikolajczyk, former Polish Prime Minister in London, announced yesterday that he is preparing a statement on the arrests.

He said that the arrested men cannot be accused of diversionary acts against the Soviet forces, as they were sincere partisans of a Polish-Soviet understanding.

Masses of Londoners stand in Whitehall to listen to Churchill's speech on VE Day.

In Downing Street, jubilant citizens celebrate victory, and the end of war.

1945

13-14 FEBRUARY The German city of Dresden is devastated, following night and day attacks by 750 RAF and 400 USAAF bombers. Some 100,000 people are killed, with another 300,000 injured, for the city was full of refugees

7 MARCH US forces cross the Rhine into Germany by seizing intact the Ludendorff Bridge at Remagen

They were up entirely and everybody came out and the House got up.

I came home; it was quite early in the day. And I said to my husband in the middle of the afternoon, 'What are we going to do?'

He said, 'What do you mean, what are we going to do?'

'Well,' I said, 'this is a most momentous day, we can't stay home.'

'Can't we?' he said, rather surprised.

'We must go up to the West End somewhere.'

'Well,' he said, 'where? It'll be so crowded.'

'Never mind, let's be in the crowd.' This is how I was that day, you see.

So we got up to Whitehall, Charing Cross. And we got through gradually. And I was underneath the Treasury balcony – thousands upon thousands of people packed tight. And you might have seen some of this in recent TV pictures – every now and again, they show it. I was standing right underneath the balcony when they shouted and shouted for Churchill. Nobody was quite certain where he was but he came out on that balcony. And it was an unrecorded speech, nobody was there to do anything. I couldn't get through to report anything afterwards.

He came out on the balcony and he flung his

11 MARCH Essen is bombed during a daylight raid made by more than 1,000 RAF bombers; the city and rail junction are crippled following the barrage of 4,700 tons of bombs

18 MARCH Berlin endures heavy bombing once again, as 4,000 bombs are dropped by Allied forces, which hit the city centre and cause major structural damage

1945

arms out. And he said, 'Londoners, I love you all,' and said a few words. He praised them for their fortitude; they had won the war, he said. He thanked them all; it was short and sweet but lovely for the Londoners. And he finished up once more: 'Londoners, I love you all!' The cheers – it was a wonder the clouds didn't come down. It was a really most momentous occasion. And no photographers there at all. It was unexpected – they didn't know where he was.

Now we, after that, managed to get through the short end towards the Houses of Parliament and then got round and got home. But that to me is the most outstanding day of my time reporting Parliament, starting with Churchill in the morning and that late at night.

Revellers in London's West End celebrate VE Day walking along Piccadilly blowing party trumpets.

Lilias Woolven was eighteen on VE Day.

I remember the end of the war very clearly, the announcement being made on the radio that at such and such a time the war would be over. Where people had got the stuff from I don't know, but there were bonfires immediately and everybody drew back their curtains and every single light in the house was put on because, of course, no lights were allowed during the war.

In 1939 the death of a score of people in an air raid by a handful of bombers was shocking. By

1945

23 MARCH British and Canadian forces cross the Rhine, supported by airborne landings

27 MARCH The last V-2 rocket launched at the UK lands in Orpington, Kent; 2,754 civilians have been killed by V-2s, 6,523 have been seriously injured

1943 1,000-bomber raids were commonplace. The Second World War had brought the front line to everyone. **Jean Mills:**

> In the olden days you used to send the men off to war and the women to sit at home and roll bandages. I think this time it was just as much the civilian population involved as the servicemen.

The war in Europe was over, but the war in the Far East against the Empire of Japan was not. The United States was making plans for an invasion of the Japanese mainland in 1946.

There had been a shadow over VE Day for **Rosamond Boddy:**

The scene of devastation in Hiroshima in the aftermath of the atomic bomb. (IWM: MH 29447)

> I think everyone, a bit, thought that the war in Japan was going on and that people who were in Europe would be sent to the Far East. So although we were glad we weren't going to be bombed any more, that was really our only thankfulness. We had an awful feeling that people were going to be sent out to the Far East. Which fortunately didn't happen because of the Bomb.

On 6 August 1945 there was another raid on Japan. But it did not summon up a vast swarm of planes. Just three giant American B29 bombers flew to Hiroshima. One, the *Enola Gay*, carried Little Boy, the first operational atomic bomb. It was dropped at 8.16 a.m. Tens of thousands of people died instantly. Birds ignited in flight. By the end of the year the total of dead was estimated at 100,000.

29 MARCH The last V-1 flying bomb to land in the UK hits Kent; 6,184 civilians have been killed by V-1s, 17,981 seriously injured

15 APRIL British troops liberate the Bergen-Belsen concentration camp in north-eastern Germany

1945

140

24 APRIL Hitler's Berchtesgaden mountain retreat is targeted in the last significant raid over Germany by RAF Bomber Command

30 APRIL Adolf Hitler commits suicide

6 AUGUST First operational atomic bomb dropped on Hiroshima, 80,000 people die outright

9 AUGUST Second atomic bomb dropped on Nagasaki, killing 40,000 people immediately

The reaction in the Allied countries was incredulity and horror and – hope.

Rosamond Boddy:

When the war was over, it was marvellous. It was a terrific relief. We could get on with our lives.

In 1942 and 1943 **Eleanor Hudson's** paintings had been exhibited at the National Gallery. But there was always her other war work, in the last full year of the Second World War.

I was doing my mobile canteen to various places around Kensington wherever these flying bombs came down and there was this square where these very beautiful trees – in late summer I think it was – were so blasted they were lost in a fog of dust. I saw stark – like trees in winter, every leaf – they had been in full leaf – every leaf was blown off. And it was sad to see this, this wrecked square covered, as in snow almost, with the blast, the dust and the bare trees. I was so delighted a month later or two to realize that there was another spring in very late summer or early autumn. The trees hadn't finished their life and they had put out new leaves. I thought it was a delightful miracle.

A mushroom cloud from the second atomic bomb rises over Nagasaki, Japan. (IWM: MH 2629)

The Thames is illuminated by floodlights and a firework display as VE Day celebrations continue into the night.

15 AUGUST VJ Day – a speech recorded by the Japanese Emperor on 14 August, declaring unconditional surrender, is broadcast to the Japanese nation. The threat of further atomic attacks and certain land defeat by the Soviets combined to ensure Japan's capitulation

The Voices – list of contributors

Stanley Baron 8877/4
Tony Bartley 11086/3
Roland Beamont 10128/10129
Rosamond Boddy 9078/3
Francis Codd 9341
Jean Conan Doyle 15795
Anne Duncan 9995/4
Hugh Dundas 10159/2
Lily Dytham 7262/2
Harold Gower 10966
John Graham 8337
William Gregory 11545/4
Ellen Harris 9820
Eric Hill 12673
Klaus Hinrichsen 003789/09
Rosemary Horstmann 10871/2
Vera Howard 14993
Eleanor Hudson 6085
Reginald Lewis 9794
Jean Mills 11885/3
Ernest Munson 16779
Diana Pitt Parsons 9948/6
Elizabeth Quayle 10609/3
Colin Ryder Richardson 20805/4
Myrtle Solomon 4846
Lilias Walker (née Woolven) 13578
Frederick Winterbotham 7462
Petrea Winterbotham (née Grant) 7463

The numbers are IWM classifications.

Select Bibliography

These are among the books drawn on for
The Battle of Britain and the Blitz.

Arnold-Foster, Mark, *The World at War*
(Collins, London, 1973)

Calder, Angus, *The Myth of the Blitz*
(Jonathan Cape, London. 1991)

Calder, Angus, *The People's War*
(Jonathan Cape, London, 1960)

Engelman, Bernt, *In Hitler's Germany*
(Methuen, London, 1988)

Howard, Michael, *The Invention of Peace*
(Profile Books, 2000)

Johnson, J. E. (Johnnie), *Full Circle*
(Cassell, London, 1964)

Kaplan, Philip, and Collier, Richard, *The Few*
(Seven Dials, Cassell, London, 1989)

Lewin, Ronald, *Ultra Goes to War*
(Hutchinson, London, 1978)

Michel, Jean, *Dora* (J. C. Lattès, Livre de poche, Paris,
1975; Weidenfeld & Nicolson, London, 1979)

Middlebrook, Martin, *The Nuremberg Raid* (Allen
Lane, Penguin Books, London, 1973, revised 1980)

Overy, Richard, *The Battle of Britain*
(Penguin Books, London, 2000)

Purnell's History of the Second World War (1966)

Rhodes, Richard, *The Making of the Atomic Bomb*
(Simon & Schuster, 1986)

Shirer, William L., *The Rise and Fall of the Third Reich*
(Simon & Schuster, New York, 1960)

Shute, Neville, *What Happened to the Corbetts*
(Heinemann, London, 1939)

Taylor, A. J. P., *English History 1914–1945*
(Oxford University Press, Oxford, 1965)

Terkel, Studs, *The Good War* (Pantheon Books, 1984)

Warner, Philip, *The Battle of France 1940*
(Cassell, London, 2001)

Wood, Derek, and Dempster, Derek, *The Narrow
Margin* (Hutchinson, London, 1961)

CD music credits and acknowledgements

Sound effects used courtesy of the Imperial War Museum Sound Archive.

Musical extracts used courtesy of River Records.

Noel Coward: 'London Pride' – taken from *Favourite Songs That Won The War* (RRCD06/IWM)

Carroll Gibbons: 'Fools Rush In' – taken from *Forces Romance* (RRCD35/IWM)

Vera Lynn: 'The White Cliffs Of Dover' – taken from *Our Finest Hour* (RRCD03/IWM)

Vera Lynn: 'A Nightingale Sang In Berkeley Square' – taken from *Forces Romance* (RRCD35/IWM)

All titles available from the Imperial War Museum (Tel: 020 7416 5000)

CD interviewees

Stanley Baron
Tony Bartley
Roland Beamont
Francis Codd
Anne Duncan
Hugh Dundas
Harold Gower
John Graham
William Gregory
Ellen Harris
Rosemary Horstmann
Eleanor Hudson
Jean Mills
Ernest Munson
Diana Pitt Parsons
Elizabeth Quayle
Colin Ryder Richardson

143